Roger Brown: A Life

ROGER BROWN:
A LIFE

bioGraph LLC

Published by bioGraph
Chicago, IL
bioGraphbook.com

First bioGraph edition April 2021

For information about discounts for bulk purchases,
please contact info@bioGraphbook.com

Cover and Book Design by bioGraph
Manufactured in the United States of America
2 3 4 5 6 7 8 9 10

Printed on 100gsm white paper

Library of Congress Control Number: 2021904604

ISBN: 978-1-951946-13-5 (Hardcover)
ISBN: 978-1-951946-16-6 (Paperback)

To all Brown family members,
past, present and future.

CONTENTS

A Note from Roger   vii

Our Known Universe   1

On His Way   35

From Fairest Creatures   63

Luxury and Thrift   95

Golden Age   133

Epilogue   169

Selected Letters   175

A NOTE FROM ROGER

Why write a biography? Who cares? What difference can it make? I have been thinking about doing this for a very long time. The idea penetrated my skull when a family office investment advisor kept suggesting I should record my story. I resisted the thought for many months as the prospect of rereading all my weekly letters and extensive travel diaries overwhelmed any urge to start the process. Regardless, encouragement from some children and grandchildren kept the idea alive. After all, I don't have many more years to live and I recall that my father was 90 (I am now 95) when he began writing *Reminiscences*. Maybe I can document some thoughts before it's too late.

A FAMILY PORTRAIT

February 1931, Cortez Street, Chicago

Isidore with a Pince-nez, Howard, Roger, & Gladys

Chapter 1

OUR KNOWN UNIVERSE

ROGER BROWN'S NAME INSPIRES RESPECT in Chicago business and philanthropy. He has the reputation of a trailblazer, with a hand in creating some of Chicago's most enduring financial institutions, including the Chicago Board Options Exchange and Harris Associates. His son Andrew recalled that Roger "could pick up his telephone and call a wide range of people from all walks of life, and they'd pick it up because it was Roger Brown calling." The patriarch of a large clan, he was the beloved husband of Barbara Brown for more than sixty years. His story appears classically American: the grandson of immigrants making a fortune, moving to the suburbs, and peacefully enjoying the esteem of his family and colleagues in his final years.

In many ways, this *is* Roger's story; this book recounts innovation, achievement, and domestic happiness. But this is no hagiography: Roger is no saint. As Roger himself wrote in "Confessions," an autobiographical sketch intended as a prospectus for this book,

> I must admit to a strong egocentric and selfish tendency in many of the things I think about, and many that I do. Of course my financial successes benefitted family members, but I think that my children might have preferred me to be more attentive to their activities.

In the weekly letters he wrote to his family, his mood often turned reflective: self-criticism creeping into otherwise routine announcements of travels, tennis matches, and family gatherings. Those who knew Roger best—his sons Jeffrey, Owen, Andy, and Henry, and his daughter Vanessa—caution against overstressing these expressions of self-doubt. Though he could be cynical, Roger was more pragmatic than philosophical.

Complications marked Roger's family life. His parenting style was a mix of affection and sometimes bitter teasing: his jibes painful to the extent that, in 2000, his family staged an intervention at Northmoor Country Club in Highland Park, Illinois, asking him to soften his tone. As Gary Holzman, executive director of the Brown's family office, noted in an interview with bioGraph, Roger was unaware of the harm he had caused.

"I can't believe you sat through that. I would've gotten up and just said, 'To heck with you guys' and backed out," Gary remembers telling Roger, as they left the meeting.

"No, no, they're entitled to their feelings," Roger replied, "I didn't realize that was what was happening."

This biography does not dwell on such moments, nor does it romanticize Roger—or exaggerate his self-awareness. Rather than lionize some generic titan of industry, we observe the man in his own writing and attempt to be objective, honest, and, where necessary, critical. Our aim is to represent Roger's successes and humanity, alongside his failures and foibles. As Owen reflected,

> *Roger was happy with what he accomplished, which was to grow rich, raise a family, help others. He was rooted in mid-century optimism, and felt, through much of his life, that opportunity abounded. He was*

also deeply fatalistic (what he would call realistic)
about new ventures, about his children's talents,
or lack of them, and the future of the American
commonwealth. An unusual mix!

A VERY SPECIAL HUMAN BEING

Roger was born on December 22, 1925 at Lying-In Hospital, now part of the University of Chicago's Hospital. His family was living in the Ukrainian Village, then an immigrant neighborhood on the West Side of Chicago. Its population was a motley mix of Poles, Jews, and other recent transplants from eastern Europe. The Brown family was one of those newly arrived.

Hirsch and Amelia Brown, Roger's grandparents, had immigrated—twice—in the 1880s. They were from the towns of Gollub and Dobrzyn, separated by the Drwęca River; one in Poland, the other in Russia. They came first in 1883, two years after the assassination of Tsar Alexander II in 1881. Nominally liberal, Alexander reformed the moribund agricultural society of 19th century Russia. In 1861, he emancipated the serfs. He abolished the military schools established by his father, Nicholas I, where Jewish youths were forced to adopt the Eastern Orthodox faith. He allowed Jews to matriculate at high schools and universities; in the late 1850s and 1860s, he permitted certain Jews to settle beyond the Pale of Settlement. These were small freedoms, especially compared to the relative economic and political liberty that Jews enjoyed in Western Europe. But Alexander's assassination ended this modest experiment in Jewish

TODDLER ROGER
Circa 1933
On the beach

freedom. A wave of violent pogroms ensued, along with the anti-Semitic May Laws, a "temporary" measure that remained on the books for more than thirty years. Forced conscriptions resumed. Jews flooded from the country, fearing for their lives.

Hirsch and Amelia Brown were among the initial wave. We may speculate on their feelings about building a new life in a foreign tongue and nation; whatever their emotions upon arriving in America, they quickly abandoned the project and returned to Gollub and Dobrzyn. According to Isidore, Roger's father, Amelia didn't like the New World.

However, Hirsch and Amelia returned to America in 1887. They stayed with Hirsch's cousin, Sam Brown, in Buffalo for a few months, working in his tailor shop and living in a small room behind it. They already had five children, on their way to eight. Their sixth, Isidore, was born in Buffalo, the first of their children born on American soil.

In 1895, the Browns moved to Chicago. Hirsch came a few months before his wife and children. He found work as a street peddler, selling fruits and vegetables. His modest income afforded occasional luxuries. Isidore recalls begging his father for a $1 hat at his bar mitzvah—a significant sum in the period. Hirsch emerges in *Reminiscences*, Isidore's memoir, as a resourceful figure, even if he never achieved the professional eminence or financial security that Isidore and Roger later attained. He worked as a tailor, a grocer, and a junk seller. He was tall, well-built, and strong: Isidore called him "husky."

He had to negotiate a complex and contradictory city. Two years before he arrived, Chicago hosted the World's Fair, a kind of debut for the young metropolis: its gleaming, neoclassical pavilions announcing the city as a rival to New York. Downtown, the first steel frame skyscrapers rose from the city's swampy soil—like Holabird and Roche's Marquette Building at the corner of Dearborn and Adams, completed the year Hirsch arrived in the city. On the river, a rougher set of monuments took root, such as the craggy, immense Montgomery Ward Warehouse, begun in 1906. In Chicago such things were possible: the marriage of daring feats of engineering with a distinctively American aesthetic.

Yet, Chicago was a city of the industrial revolution, with the attendant ills. The miasma of the stockyards hung in the air; the river teemed with steamers unloading goods; lofty architecture soared above settlement houses full of immigrant families. There is no evidence that the Browns endured this level of poverty, but the everyday life of Isidore and his brothers was closer to the settlement house than the skyscraper. The family slept four to a bed to stay warm; they had no electricity. Isidore stole kosher pickles from his rabbi—a delicacy in those days—and pennies from the collection box for Jews in Palestine. He joined his fathers and brothers at work early, selling newspapers on the street. He drove the family cart to market and delivered groceries to poor families around the neighborhood. The family's horse was blind, so Isidore tramped through the streets, guiding it by its bridle.

Faced with such poverty, Isidore's family realized that education was the key to improving the family's fortunes.

But Isidore was not a dedicated student: "I admit I was never known as a scholar," he reminisced. His father and brothers pushed him, sometimes physically, through high school and college: "I did just enough schoolwork to get by, and tried to quit on several occasions. My father and my older brother, Jacob, quite literally clubbed me into capitulating, and I stayed on until I finished"—eventually earning a law degree. Roger remembered, "My father, Isidore, was what I would call a political attorney. He was an effective attorney, but he had friends at City Hall that would get things done." That "but" is telling: in the Chicago of those years, having friends in the right places was more important than your legal skills.

Isidore was an unlikely, contradictory, mix. His temper was legendary in the family. Yet, Roger also admired his father's decisive intelligence: "Isidore was an aggressive attorney, had good political relationships, was a guy who thought quickly and acted quickly. If he had an idea—*boom*—he started executing it. He didn't sit around and try to figure out optimal ways of doing everything. That proved to be a very successful formula for him." He was decisive yet reflective; as Roger recalled, he was "also interested in literature and Shakespeare. And after working in the office, he'd come home, and he would sit in a big blue chair and read: sometimes business work, other times pleasure."

In 1915, he met Gladys Jordan, "a very special human being" with "liquid brown eyes." She had been in Chicago for less than a decade, having arrived on Saint Patrick's Day in 1907. As a result, Isidore always had a soft spot for the holiday. Gladys' father had been a grocer in Ohio. When he died, she and her mother moved west to be closer to family in Chicago. Isidore and Gladys' families had known each other in the old country; the two interacted casually on social occasions. When he left home to serve in World War I, Isidore gave Gladys a gold pen with his initials engraved on it. He sent her love notes daily, "dressing up my letters with lines of poetry that I borrowed from the classics." By the end of the war, he had won her.

In Isidore's memoirs and Roger's memories, Gladys cut a charismatic figure. Isidore praised her dancing and recalled her being elected to play the lead role, the queen, in an elementary school play. As Isidore reflected on his youth in his nineties, Gladys retained a majestic aura. For Roger, too, her memory retained its living vibrancy into his ninth decade. As Roger recalled in an interview with bioGraph, Gladys "was really a unique personality; the kind of person who could walk into a hotel that had no available rooms and convince them to give her one. She was a very attractive person, and I don't think she had an enemy in the world."

"As you might guess," Isidore vaunted, "such a beautiful and charming girl as my Gladys had many suitors vying for her favor." He named his vanquished rivals: Elmer E. Mills, Arthur Schoenstadt, Louis Widran, and, the most serious source of consternation, Mike Greenberg. Isidore quashed these competitors with his charm and knack for romantic gifts, such as the box of red American Beauty roses he sent Gladys for her twenty-third birthday.

They were engaged in 1919 over a light luncheon at Krantz's on State Street across from Marshall Field's. At

A PICTURE OF ELEGANCE
Early 1930s
Gladys

the time, their position was precarious; even procuring an engagement ring presented financial obstacles: "I begged, borrowed, earned—indeed, all but stole enough money to buy a beautiful diamond solitaire." They were married on October 9, 1920 in a small ceremony at Temple Beth-El, a reform temple on the Northwest side. They couldn't afford a honeymoon, so they spent three nights at the Blackstone Hotel. Isidore promised to make it up to Gladys—a promise he kept. "When I look at the globe," he wrote in his later years, reflecting on their travels, "I see that we have visited virtually every major country with the exception of China (and there we've landed in Hong Kong and Kowloon)."

As newlyweds, Isidore and Gladys moved into an apartment on the second floor of a three-flat at 2333 West Cortez Avenue. In 1923, after three years of married life, they welcomed their first child, Howard. Roger followed two years later. "Roger and I have one sterling credential," Howard remarked nearly seventy years later, in a 1991 speech celebrating his brother's career: "We showed eminent good taste in the choice of our parents. Nor are you aware of the fact that our parents preferred daughters. I was to be named Bernice; Roger, Patricia. But fate, that most tyrannical of despots, decreed otherwise."

To help care for the children, Isidore hired a nurse, Miss Lyons. In *Reminiscences*, he recorded quotidian details of this time, including her lullabies: "You are your mother's joy, / A perfect baby boy." Isidore also remembered a curious habit from Roger's infancy: each night, Roger would knock his head forcefully against the headboard of his crib. Efforts to restrain the determined infant were unsuccessful. "At the worst," Isidore commented, "he must have been drumming some brains *into* his head."

The apartment was a standard Chicago railroad apartment—long and narrow, with living room, dining room, and bedroom branching off its central hallway. From the back porch, the young brothers could watch the ice man come up the alley to fill their icebox. During an interview with bioGraph, Roger slipped into a reverie—closing his eyes and recalling the details of the space: "In the dining room, we had a dining room table and my brother used to chase me, or I used to chase my brother, around the table. My brother's two and a half years older. I think he used to take advantage of me a bit."

Howard was known as the "nice one." Roger was "the nice looking one." Howard would greet aunts and uncles, as expected. Roger was less polite, repelled by their Yiddish accents. In photos from this time, Howard smiles while Roger glowers at the camera. Of course, Howard also joined Roger in pranks; for example, locking their aunts Gertrude and Mae on the fire escape, a jape that earned the boys a whipping. Gladys once locked them in the back stairwell after she caught them fighting.

Roger's intransigence sometimes resulted in special punishment. He was barred from attending the 1936 Olympic trials at the University of Chicago because he, first, insulted his Hebrew teacher, second, refused to practice piano, and third, dropped a paper bag full of water on the head of a classmate who lived next door. Roger's delinquency cost dearly: as a result, he missed seeing Jesse Owens in person, while well-behaved Howard watched the "Buckeye Bullet" qualify for the Berlin Olypmics.

Between these episodes of delinquency, Roger was a careful observer of his family's circumstances on Cortez Avenue, and began to formulate his foundational ambition: he wanted to be rich. He watched Isidore's siblings struggle financially, slipping in and out of poverty. As Roger wrote in his "Confessions," their struggles "influenced my desire to become rich, so that I would not find myself in their circumstances." Isidore's brothers, Jacob and Philip, had helped him through school, selling candy for him in movie theaters. Once Isidore was established in his law practice, he supported them in turn, giving them cash and finding them jobs, even during the Depression. He helped his brother Jacob set up a produce business. When that failed, he got him a job as a truck driver, then as a clerk in the Cook County Recorder's Office. In doing so, Isidore was fulfilling a familial obligation, not seeking recognition: "Mind you, I didn't work for them to win their love. With me, it was a simple matter of duty."

Not just fear of penury but also desire for success propelled Roger. In a letter from the 1990s, he meditates on the uncanny sympathy he felt with Ron Chernow's history of the Warburg family, a prominent Jewish-German banking family: "I didn't realize that I could read so much about a family that I would never meet and really never know. But in many ways their tremendous business successes are what I fantasized about even before I started work in the securities business."

Nor were these idle fantasies: even as a child, Roger paid acute and precocious attention to his father's business dealings. During the Depression, Isidore purchased a hotel on Jackson Boulevard in downtown Chicago. The man who leased the hotel, Mr. Bernstein, was unable to keep the hotel full of paying guests and fell behind on his rent. One day, Isidore took Howard and Roger downtown to visit the hotel; Mr. Bernstein greeted them at the door and introduced himself. Having heeded Isidore's exchanges, Roger demanded, "Is this the man who owes you all the rent?" Isidore remembered: "We were terribly embarrassed and tried to pass over the boy's remark in silence. We just hadn't appreciated how keenly Roger followed our conversations about business matters."

BROWNS DON'T FLUNK

During their years on Cortez Avenue, Roger and Howard's playmates came from the neighborhood: a colorful cast of immigrant children. A young Saul Bellow—the great novelist of the Jewish west side—lived across the street, alongside an Irish family, the Bradys. Mr. Brady was a broad-shouldered Irish cop. He had four children; two around Roger and Howard's age. They watched basketball games together at the church across Oakley Boulevard. Though Roger was never big enough or old enough to play, he watched the games with enthusiasm.

Howard and Roger attended the neighborhood school, the Columbia School on Augusta Boulevard. "The big event in that school," Roger recalled, describing his daily routine as a student, "Was to be appointed to clean the blackboard erasers every day, on a blackboard eraser cleaning machine, and I think I might have done it a couple of times." Isidore and Gladys questioned the quality of education at the Columbia School. Having climbed from selling newspapers in the street to walking the corridors of City Hall, Isidore wanted to ensure that his sons kept rising. When Howard and Roger were children, he coined a maxim to motivate them: "Browns don't flunk!"

Seeking better education, Gladys and Isidore moved the family to the South Side so the boys could attend the University of Chicago Lab Schools, a private school affiliated with the university. By the standards of the day, the Lab Schools were experimental. Founded in 1896 by pragmatist philosopher John Dewey, the school rejected 19th century pedagogy, with its reliance on rote memorization. Instead, children planted gardens, played with blocks, solved problems. They learned by doing.

In his evening reading, Isidore had studied Dewey's work. He felt strongly enough about this emerging educational model that he gave up his political connections on the Northwest Side, where he was linked to the Kelly-Nash Machine. The family moved into an apartment at 5000 South Cornell Avenue, in East Hyde Park—a Jewish quarter on the eastern border of the Kenwood neighborhood. The apartment was about a mile-and-a-half from the school; Roger and Howard carpooled with other kids from the block. Later, they moved to 5715 South Kenwood Avenue, a short walk from the school.

In those years, Hyde Park was a conservative stronghold in a Democratic city. Isidore went to work flipping the district. Gladys was also politically active, helping Isidore get out the vote on election day. It was unusual for a woman to be active in politics then, particularly in Chicago's macho precinct politics: in her own way,

ISIDORE WITH ROGER & HOWARD
1931

Gladys was a pioneer of women's political involvement in American democracy.

For all Isidore's sacrifices, Roger rejected the school's pedagogy. Like his father before him, he was no scholar. As Roger described his studies in a letter from the 1970s,

> *I was lazy and undisciplined; therefore, I did not do the appropriate level of work because I got a greater kick out of solving math problems and understanding how things work from science, etc. I never understood the purpose of Latin and I had so much trouble with French that it was an anathema to me.*

Yet, even in arithmetic, Roger had to ask his deskmate, Adele Krause, to help with sums. Eventually, he abandoned the Deweyan method and started memorizing them. In seventh or eighth grade, a science teacher tried to make the class do a homework assignment every week. Roger refused. Instead, he copied his friend Bill Kornhauser's homework. As Howard later joked, "I studied with intensity to perfect my commitment to mediocrity whereas Roger never allowed his studies to interfere with his education." Gladys may have learned more than Roger did in those years: while the boys were in school, she enrolled in continuing education courses at the University of Chicago, where she focused on psychology.

While still at the Lab Schools, Roger took steps toward manhood. He was confirmed in the Jewish faith at Sinai Temple, on 48th Street in Hyde Park, in 1938. Neither he nor Howard enjoyed studying Hebrew; they burned through a series of tutors. Roger also had his first job, working as a page at American National Bank. He only worked about a month, between summer camp and the start of school. But he was required to wear long trousers for the job; Gladys bought Roger his first pair. Even while becoming a man, Roger retained the privileges of his childhood. In the 1930s, he held a job on a construction site, acquired through Isidore's connections. At the shift's end, the foreman grabbed him and said, "Kid, your limousine is outside waiting for you."

As he stepped into the world, Roger continued to be the sometimes-rowdy boy he had been in the Ukrainian Village. Shortly after the move to the South Side, he got into a scrap with neighborhood boys and, overpowered, fled into an intersection without looking; he was struck by a passing automobile. He picked himself up and went on to school. He didn't bother mentioning the incident to his parents—but the fifth ward alderman saw it and reported him. On another occasion, Roger learned that a classmate was afraid of butterflies. Howard was invited to her birthday party; Roger was added to the guest list out of a sense of social obligation. He repaid this charity by showing up with a box of butterflies. One can imagine the pandemonium when the birthday girl opened the box and the insects burst into the room.

Just as Roger arrived in high school, the new president of the University of Chicago, Robert Maynard Hutchins, decided to change the structure of the curriculum. Hutchins is now regarded as a dynamic leader, who demanded that the institutions he led lived up to their ideals. However, his curricular reforms stymied Roger: while his friends moved up to the next grade, he was held back a year.

Roger, frustrated, sought a way out—and found it in his brother's example. Howard had already quit Hyde Park and headed east, enrolling at Phillips Exeter Academy in New Hampshire. Howard had read about Exeter in an article in *Fortune* magazine; the article convinced him that the faraway school would offer the best preparation for college, and the best chance at admission to an Ivy League institution. It was difficult for Jews to attain admission to Exeter at the time; like many elite American institutions, the school imposed a quota on its Jewish students. It is Brown family lore that Gladys, by sheer force of personality, gained entrance for both Roger and Howard. Speaking to the Dean of Admissions, she is reported to have said: "If you accept my sons at Exeter, you will be just as proud of them one day as they will be of the school." Howard arrived in 1940, when he was sixteen. After a course at summer school to make up missing credits, Roger abandoned the Lab Schools and arrived the next year.

AWAY FROM HOME

Sited on the banks of the Squamscott River in southeastern New Hampshire, Exeter was not only academically demanding. It was also hard to reach from Chicago, given the primitive state of air travel in the early 1940s. Five decades later, Roger reflected on this time in a travel diary:

For a moment think about the transition of the present monumental airport facilities compared to what we experienced 57 years ago when our family flew from Midway airport to New York. I believe we landed at Newark which then was the only airport serving the N.Y. metropolitan area. This was a trip to visit the New York World's Fair and then followed by a driving trip north to visit schools for Uncle Howard...The facilities at Midway airport were quite primitive. People would come to the airport to be entertained by planes landing and taking off. Passengers felt they were celebrities and stewardesses were selected from registered nurses who applied eagerly for the jobs...Maybe our grandchildren or their children will be making similar passenger voyages into space during the next fifty years.

The trip to Exeter was far less glamorous: Roger took the New York Central rail line to Boston, and there transferred to the Boston & Maine line, a journey of several days.

By the time Roger arrived at Exeter, however, he was already an experienced traveler. His early trips inspired a life-long love for travel and for sports which were then exotic—like skiing. In 1938, Isidore and Gladys took the family to Sun Valley, Idaho for a Christmas ski trip. They were passengers on the inaugural trip of the City of Los Angeles, a cross-country train owned by the Union Pacific Railroad. En route, they stopped at a station in Idaho, where they were entertained by dances from members of a local Shoshone tribe. Howard and Roger skied the now-defunct beginner's slope, Penny Hill. There was no chairlift, only a tow rope. They took lessons from a team of Austrian ski instructors, some of whom subsequently served under Hitler. They watched the Austrians compete in ski-jumping against Alf Engen, a Norwegian Olympic champion. Isidore and Gladys enjoyed walking around the resort and listening to Edie Duchin's orchestra's evening performances.

At the time, skiing was almost unheard of in the U.S. For Roger, the trip was a thrilling introduction to the sport, which became one of his great passions. He spent on average at least ten days a year skiing for most of his adult life. In 1997, during a dinner with Marge and Bob Fridstein in Aspen, Marge observed how central skiing had been to Roger's life. Roger ruminated on the comment in his next letter to the family:

> *Funny, but I hadn't focused on this thought as I had just believed that skiing was ancillary to the key things on which I have concentrated such as family, wealth accumulation and intellectual enhancement... Subsequently, while riding up the chair lift I realize how much of life had been dedicated to such journeys and how much I had enjoyed the sport.*

In the summers, the boys were likewise active voyagers, traveling to camps in Wisconsin: first Camp Kawaga and later Camp Nawakwa. Roger was six or seven when he started going; Howard had been there the year before. Camp Kawaga was founded in 1915 by a rabbi, Doctor Ehrenreich—known to campers simply as Doc E. It was one of the first twenty-five summer camps in the country. In its early years, it had a serious educational mission; as Doc E. described it, "Fun, yes, but always with the thought of the final effect on the boy." Roger was little concerned with this educational prerogative, however. He focused instead on learning to swim and sail, then on swimming across Lake Kawaguesaga. In his second year, Roger accomplished this feat, earning the privilege of taking out canoes and rowboats in the evening. He and Howard spent their summers at camp roughhousing on the beach—sometimes too roughly: Howard began high school in a full body cast after Roger pushed him into the shallows.

THE MOTHER LODE

Roger did not relinquish his delinquency when he stepped off the Boston & Maine and through the gates of Exeter. Early in his time there, he was summoned to the Dean's Office for placing peas on a knife and slinging them at a faculty member. Howard was also arraigned, in the hopes that Roger's behavior might be amended through the influence of an older brother. The dean was stern, insisting that such behavior was unacceptable and worthy of discipline. But, he added, the real problem was with Roger's aim: he had missed the faculty member and hit his wife.

Making good on Gladys' promise to the Dean of Admissions, Roger has remained devoted to Exeter, donating to the school, sending his children there, encouraging his grandchildren to attend too. He regards

ROGER AT 15

1941, North Shore garden

With his father Isidore

Exeter as the foundation of his success—more important, in terms of the skills and habits it taught, than Yale
or Harvard Business School. As Roger wrote half a
century later,

> *Many of my better traits were learned there, formed
> under the pressure of trying to keep up with this
> group of racehorses. My experience may be sharper
> than that of my sons who attended for four years
> and did not have the contrast of transferring from
> a plodding public high school into this arena. If I
> had not gone to Exeter, I would never have gone to
> Yale or Harvard. My association with these prestige
> schools elevated my horizons and stimulated my
> growth. They made me demand more from myself
> as well as heightened anticipation by others of my
> performance. Exeter was the Mother lode.*

Challenged by his peers and the great expectations of his
teachers, Roger sloughed off his earlier scholastic lassi-
tude, developing a strong work ethic. As he wrote in a
letter from the 1970s:

> *One of the reasons that Exeter provides such a
> superior education is because of the continuous
> burden of work pressure that they exert on the
> competitive student. After a while, the unusual
> burden of a difficult problem becomes routine.
> When one encounters such problems later on in
> life, they do not appear overwhelming. They can be*

approached with equanimity by someone with a bit of experience.

Roger encountered serious challenges in his academics at Exeter, as did subsequent generations of Browns: "Everyone in our family has some kind of trouble during the first or second year at Exeter and the only solution is to recognize it at an early stage—dig in and turn it around before it turns you around," he wrote his sons. Roger himself had to stay an extra summer in order to graduate on time.

The benefits of an Exeter education transcended the classroom. Roger roomed with Otis Pease, who later became a professor of history at Washington University. When Pease visited Roger in the early 1980s, Roger reflected on their intellectual bond:

> *In reviewing my past I realize how important the combination of Otis and Exeter have been in my intellectual development... For me, Exeter was the place where my intellectual energy was unzipped and where it started to probe for the real world. This didn't happen in the classroom—it happened in the bull sessions, in the card games. Classes were a stern discipline; athletics, a physical relief for confinement; other organized activities, an opportunity to perform; but the growth was in the free, open, and wild discussions about events of the day, life, love, and all other pursuits... At Exeter I met a great variety of different persuasions and contrasting backgrounds, from different countries, different states, and varying*

socio-economic climates... The confinement of the school and the unity forced by early morning chapel, Saturday night movies and spectator attendance at key athletic and extra-curricular events all mixed together with scholastic achievement melded a spirit of élan and excellence. This spirit has not been replicated in my life.

However, circumstances abroad cast a pall over the joy of bull sessions and card games. In December of 1941, Roger was a Lower Middler, living in Wheelwright House dormitory. He was playing bridge in the butt room when someone rushed down to give the news: the Japanese had struck Pearl Harbor. As he wrote later, reflecting on the moment,

It was unbelievable. How could those little oriental idiots have the gall to take on the U.S.? It was like Napoleon invading Russia—a no-win situation. Little did we realize or appreciate the fact that the Japanese army was, for its size, the best army in the world at that time or that the Japanese skills and culture were perfectly oriented toward successful military achievement. Well, we learned a lesson in war... I think the lesson we should have learned is not to underrate the potential of other races or cultures.

I WAS WORTHLESS

Exeter is about as far from Pearl Harbor as an American can get without leaving the continental United States. Yet the war quickly pulled Roger into its maelstrom. In his senior year, a Naval officer visited Exeter to recruit students for an officer training program, the V12. Candidates had to pass a national exam to qualify. Those who did— more than 125,000 by the end of the war—received a college education on the Navy's dime.

Roger passed the exam; the Navy sent him to Yale. After his years at Exeter, Roger's education at Yale was comparatively uninspiring. He had no desire to attend and did so only at the Navy's insistence; his heart was set on Harvard, where he planned to major in history. At Yale, Roger studied engineering without passion or enthusiasm. He had little choice; the Navy wanted engineers. The disappointment rankled. Returning to campus in the early 1980s for Henry's college graduation, Roger wrote: "Walking through the Gothic-Georgian-Modern architecture of Yale brings the question to mind whether I'll ever return. My memories of student life here are bitter, yet I admire the institution that Yale has become, and am grateful that Jeff, Owen and Henry were permitted to imbibe from its excellence."

The V12 program was grueling, intellectually and physically. Roger completed his degree in 30 months, while participating in the rituals of military training: for instance, candidates had to march regularly in uniform around campus. Each morning, they awoke to a bugle call, lined up for roll call, then jogged around the

ROGER AT YALE

May 1944, New Haven

cemetery. Reflecting on the experience in the early 1970s, Roger wrote his sons:

> *I'll never forget the first time we did it. Our battalion commander was a track man and he practically ran the rest of Davenport College to their death. Those who made it all the way back had to lay down on our bunks, sweating profusely and praying that our lungs were big enough to get air back into our systems. After a while we became inured to the run and also got a slower leader.*

Other candidates flunked out under the pressure, including several of Roger's roommates. But Roger persevered. "I didn't like it," he recalled, "but I was able to keep up with the pressure and I didn't quit." He graduated in 1945, at the age of 19—a full three years before Howard, who had entered Princeton in 1942 but had his college career interrupted by the war. Roger had been in school continuously since September 1940, with no break longer than two weeks, enduring a demanding schedule, a rigorous program of physical training, and an uninspiring curriculum.

Prejudices of classmates compounded these challenges. Like Exeter, Yale remained an anti-Semitic institution, from its admissions quotas to the attitude of its students. As Roger wrote, "We were considered 'foreigners' by the deeply traditional WASP establishment at Yale and we resented this attitude."

Though others judged him by it, Roger himself did not identify strongly with his Jewish background. When asked in early 2020 what he believes in, he scoffed, "Vodka." However, Roger conceded that anti-Semitism had marked his life. In his 1994 letter on Chernow's history of the Warburg family, Roger wrote, "I have found this book especially poignant because I have and have had some of the same compulsions. One feels like a multiple personality always supersensitive to the reaction of the Jewish and non-Jewish communities. One is governed not only by what is right or politically/economically sound, but also how it will be looked at because of one's religious affiliation."

As he finished at Yale, Roger injured his shoulder. The Navy sent him to St. Albans Hospital in New York to recover. "This was a very interesting experience," Roger reflected, "because we had guys in the ward where I was who were shot up from Guadalcanal and Peleliu and all those awful places. They were shooting full of penicillin every day." After he recovered, the Navy sent Roger back to Yale to monitor and advise younger students in the V12 program. In this period, with his duties somewhat less stringent than during his thirty-month sprint through the college, he immersed himself in the social world of Yale—for instance, trying, unsuccessfully, to join the private club at Mory's Restaurant: it was so crowded that he could only use the facilities as a guest.

His commission, when it arrived, sent him to the Pacific theater: first to San Francisco and Seattle, later to China, where he was assigned to a destroyer escort. Japanese suicide bombers often targeted these ships. It was a dangerous mission—or it would've been, had he arrived earlier. By the time Roger finished at Yale and his shoulder healed, the war was ending. Describing his maritime career in a recent interview, he indulged in self-deprecation: "I was on that ship for, I don't know, eight or nine months. If most of the officers of the Navy were like me, we would all be speaking Japanese—because I was worthless." At the time, Roger regarded his failings as a Naval Officer with regret. As he told his parents shortly after he returned from the Pacific, "Once I got in the Navy and had the opportunity to show my true ability and how outstanding I was among other officers, I fluffed off and did a rotten job."

Howard also served in World War II: he was sent first to Fort Benning, then to the University of Nebraska to study German, before finally, as a member of a two-man bazooka team, shipping out to France with the 44th Infantry Division. There he eventually ran into Colonel Albert Langeluttig—one of Isidore's business partners back in Chicago. Langeluttig saw to it that Howard received a safe assignment where he could use the languages for which the Army had originally schooled him. For the rest of his life, Howard hesitated to describe his experiences in the war, especially to his children.

Roger was eventually discharged in San Diego and sent to the Great Lakes Naval Base. He stayed in the Naval Reserves for a few more years. Returning from a ski vacation in the early 1950s, he found a package waiting for him from the Navy. It was so big it could hardly fit in the mailbox. Assessing it, he said to himself, "My God, they're calling me back for the Korean War." Then he opened it and discovered, instead, discharge papers. "I don't know how they figured out the discharge because I'd never really paid the Navy back for what they gave me," Roger confessed, "but I didn't argue. I was out and I didn't ever even want to associate with the reserve, while some of my classmates became admirals. Let them have it."

Roger's experience in World War II inspired an abiding skepticism about war. When the conflict in Vietnam ended in 1973, he expressed relief that his sons had escaped the draft, and their own brush with war:

> *Hopefully, none of you will have to join the Armed Forces for any war anymore—but history keeps telling us that we are still humans and subject to some incalculable urge to slaughter each other and wreck civilization. No one has ever been able to isolate this virus and eradicate or domesticate it. And with this grave failing we go on to knowingly destroy the most magnificent development of our known universe—the human being. Why are we so stupid, so selfish, so righteous, so honorable?*

IN UNIFORM

May 1944, Yale

Roger with Isidore

ROGER AT THE END OF HIS EXETER YEARS

1943, Chicago

Chapter 2
ON HIS WAY

ROGER SPENT THE YEAR AFTER he left the Navy back at Yale, living in a boarding house on Edgewood Street, taking classes in American Literature and History on the GI Bill. This was a way to balance his education: his studies under the V12 program had focused on engineering, which, as Andrew noted, "he couldn't have cared less about." However, in letters from the time, Roger expressed no greater enthusiasm for these liberal studies. As he told his parents in the winter of 1947, "The feeling of returning to school was terrible. No matter what I say or do, I realize that I am not a student, and I do not enjoy studying."

In his final year at Yale, Roger explored an unpromising set of prospects for the future. In the same letter from the winter of 1947, he wrote:

> *I can think of no time in my life during which I have accomplished a worthwhile task by beginning it, and finishing it with a constant push of energy in which I unfold all the blind alleys. I may start with a burst of enthusiasm or end with a burst of necessity; but seldom do I do a good job and hardly ever my best...* *My main drawback is that I DO NOT KNOW WHAT I WANT TO DO, AND IF I DID KNOW WHAT I WANTED TO DO, I WOULD NOT KNOW WHY I SHOULD DO IT.*

The proximate cause of this somber letter was a lunch meeting with a businessman named Polacheck—a friend of Isidore's—and his wife. Impressed, Roger wrote:

> *Mr. Polacheck is a very wise man who has made a fortune through his own intelligence, hard work and energy. His whole life has been based on two strong feelings: the belief that he was created on earth for some purpose, and a strong artistic interest in metal work. These two feelings were so strong that they were able to combine and build him a fortune from nothing.*

Roger measured himself against Polacheck: "I am as intelligent as John Polacheck, I am better educated than he was, and I have already been given an incipient fortune; but I don't have the drive and the inner makings that he had, or at least I have not realized them within the last twenty-one years." In response, Isidore and Gladys sent letters reassuring Roger; in his next missive he objected to their judgment of his character. On January 16, 1947, he wrote, "I really think that you love me as a son to such a great degree that you fail in a more rational analysis."

Despite their gloomy tone, these letters found Roger voicing ambitions: "I intend to get a job with a concern that is the leader in its field, but which also offers opportunities for individualism and advancement. I want to learn the industry from the biggest and the best, and then when the opportunity comes along, I want to step out and work for myself." Roger framed his goal in terms of individual achievement rather than the accumulation of wealth. Yet, as he complained to his parents, that left him in a "rather poor position, for there is only one thing that I feel qualified and able to do, and that is achieve prestige by making money." Wealth did not impress Roger as a metric of success:

> *Wealth does not compare to the internal feeling of some real and actual value. You or I may amass a fortune in money, and in that way we might assume that we achieve success. But after the first million dollars, the succeeding millions don't mean as much... And is not life one grand, envious attempt to outdo or imitate those whom you consider better? Doesn't everyone wish that he could be himself without the constant restraining bonds of the putrefying society that we live in? In short, neither you nor I know or can know what personal success is, for if we knew what personal success was, we would know the purpose of life. Therefore, we must throw away the whole idea of success and substitute a quality that is humanly measurable.*

Money couldn't sate the ambitions that, for Roger, defined the purpose of life itself. Still, he aspired toward wealth to protect his family from poverty.

Writing his future, Roger stood on the shoulders, and often in the shadows, of his father's generation: philanthropic businessmen like Julius Rosenwald and Henry Crown. Of his own father, Roger recorded, "He raised himself from nothing. He did the underlying work to make my brother and myself rich, although we did a lot of the work." By contrast, Roger and his brother grew up comfortable and privileged, with access to the most prestigious academic institutions in the country. According to Betsy Brown, Roger's sister-in-law, Howard and Roger "were boys of privilege. Isidore didn't start his life as one of privilege, but these boys did. They had known privilege all their lives." Roger recognized as much in 1947, writing to his parents, "There is nothing of great ability needed to continue making money once you have a small fortune put in your lap, the interest on which, in itself ought to be four or five times greater than my financial needs for the next five or ten years."

As a young man, Roger neither romanticized his privilege nor aggrandized himself. In a letter from Yale, he reflects, "If one were to look at my life from a complete stranger's point of view, he would say that this boy has achieved something... But when I consider these accomplishments, there is hardly anything in the whole of my life that I can consider to be more than twenty to thirty percent of my own doing." Instead, Roger celebrated the "people who have pushed me along on the right track." He also credited them for his shortcomings: "many of my failings will be due in the same proportion to these people."

THE GREAT PARADOX IN MY LIFE

That winter at Yale, Roger wrote to his parents, "The great paradox in my life is the realization within myself that I am happiest when I am working hard and doing things, yet I do the least to fulfill this realization." As he wrote the sentence, however, he was already working to solve the paradox.

A family friend had attended Harvard Business School and encouraged Roger to apply. Roger did not at first feel—or admit—excitement at the prospect. "I intend to send in an application," he informed Gladys and Isidore, "but at the present moment I do not intend to go to Harvard, because I think that going there would be just a delay in time, and it would not help to inculcate the necessary drive or feeling that are necessary for success." Still, Roger applied himself to the task, agonizing over his academic record and whom to ask for a letter of recommendation: "My marks were not too good last term, and I am more skeptical than ever about my chances for admission to the business school...There is really no businessman who knows my work, and as a matter of fact I have no military superior or teacher at school that could do a fair job in writing a recommendation." Readying himself for rejection, Roger planned to enter the workforce in the summer of 1947: "The whole situation looks rather poor, and it looks as though there is very little that I can do to ameliorate my position."

These self-criticisms were unearned: his grades were strong; Isidore worked behind the scenes to secure a letter of recommendation from Henry Crown. Roger was admitted to Harvard without much ado. As Roger wrote in 1975, advising his son Jeffrey after a mediocre academic performance, "I didn't know I wanted to go to Harvard when I was at Yale, but such options were open to me because I had an adequate record."

In succeeding years, business schools have become a fact of life: every university has one, following a more or less standard curriculum. When Roger arrived at Harvard in the fall of 1947, however, the Business School was still an unusual institution. Founded in 1908, the school pioneered a novel approach to training leaders. The education transcended textbook abstraction. It was practical, focused on corporate strategy, and grounded in real-world case studies. The professors were not academics but businessmen with experience running companies and investing in the market. They sidelined topics that occupy contemporary students—like trade, corporate culture, or international finance. Instead, the program anticipated the challenges Roger's generation would face as nascent corporate leaders. Since so many had died in the war, his peers were hurled early into leadership roles. Harvard prepared them for those responsibilities.

Roger's peers in the class of '49 were all men, the overwhelming majority of them white. Of the 652, almost all were veterans; most studied on the GI Bill. Many had seen far graver action than Roger had, flying fighter planes in the European theater or landing on beaches in the South Pacific. With a few exceptions—including Lester Crown and an Indian prince who had his servants carry his books to class—they were middle class, from families that had struggled through the Depression and the war years.

They entered the workforce just as America was entering an unprecedented industrial boom, which many rode to distinguished careers. After his 30th reunion, Roger wrote to his children, "It is amazing how many alumni (including your father) are entrepreneurial—run

ROGER DEMOBBED

1948, Harvard

their own businesses and work for themselves. Some, of course, manage multi-national companies that are gigantic in scope and others fulfill important tasks within these companies." Roger's distinguished classmates included James E. Burke of Johnson & Johnson, Charles Peter McColough of Xerox, and Marvin S. Traub of Bloomingdale's.

Harkening back to a time of integrity and innovation in American business, the class of '49 has inspired laudatory and nostalgic books. Roger shared the admiration that has attached to his cohort. "We had a great class in the business school," he affirmed, "They had some really outstanding men." But then Roger lifted the curtain on this elite mythology: "A couple of our guys were really great at publicity, and they were so good that *Fortune* magazine published an article about our class, and a book was written, and so on and so forth. Everybody thought we were geniuses." As Lawrence Shames writes, "The Business School would make successes of the guys who didn't need the Business School to succeed."

The class of '49 formed abiding friendships. They shared apartments together in New York after graduation; they attended each other's weddings; they vacationed together. Roger generally avoided such fraternizing: his Harvard classmates do not recur in his subsequent writing as do his friends from Exeter. Attending Harvard Business School cured Roger's residual regrets about having been sent to Yale by the Navy. Yet Roger later resisted engaging with Harvard, skipping his 50th reunion, despite or because of the public relations frenzy around the event. Roger's letters never dwell on his time at Harvard—while they often celebrate Exeter. To be fair, Gladys had promised Exeter, not Harvard, that Roger would one day be a proud alumnus; his children followed him to Exeter, not Harvard. Further, unlike many of his classmates, Roger did not remain out east after graduation. By the time he left Harvard Business School, he had been on the East Coast for years, first at Exeter, then Yale, then Harvard. He was ready to come home—and to move beyond the Ivy League world that had shaped him.

UNEXPECTED LOCAL INFLUENCES

In the fall of 1975, Roger wrote to his children with career advice:

> Now that each of you is starting a new year in school it should theoretically be a good time to take stock of your present activities and interests to determine your future course of endeavor. Unfortunately, the answers to the future do not light up with neon intensity to point out the direction of one's life. Very few people encounter "burning bushes" while avoiding Pharaoh's police in the desert. Most careers and choices seem determined by geographical location, unexpected local influences, and chance occurrences that are randomly activated and completely unpredictable.

On the one hand, Roger remarked the force of circumstance in shaping a career. On the other, he urged his children to discover their personal spheres of influence:

However, in spite of the appearance that all your desires and activities are completely unguided, one should not ignore many of the general directions influenced in terms of choosing schools, courses, extra-curricular activities, sports and friends. All of these tend to filter out extraneous activities and imperceptibly concentrate your efforts into areas that you have preferred.

This wisdom sprang from Roger's experience, though he often ascribed his success to luck; as his granddaughter Nicola noted, "He always says that he is very lucky!" Roger himself confessed, "I have never had a plan in my life. My important decisions were made one after another with no idea on how they would fulfill any longer-term goals. What success I have had comes from a series of lucky choices since the time I was a student in high school."

Accordingly, Roger graduated from Harvard Business School in the spring of 1949 without a clear plan for his future: "I didn't know what the hell I wanted to do after the business school." His classmates moved into prestigious—and stable—careers. "For many of them," Andrew reflected, "the big, coveted job was to go work for General Motors or General Electric or Dow Chemical or DuPont or something similar to that. And their intent and desire was to say, 'Well I'm going to go start working for that company and I'm going to work my way up until I run the company.'"

Roger took a different path. Lucy Brown, Roger's niece, speculated "that after business school he probably had many choices of places to go. But it was important to him to stay in the Chicago area." Lucy wondered "if one of the reasons that after Harvard Business School Roger chose to come back home was to be near his parents." If so, self-interest as well as filial devotion motivated Roger's homecoming. In New York, he would've been alone, without a robust network. In Chicago, he was the son of a well-connected lawyer.

The Chicago of the mid-1940s lacked the dynamism that Hirsch encountered when he arrived in the mid-1890s. As Thomas Dyja writes in his history of the city, postwar Chicago suffered a crisis of confidence in its own future: "Chicago still hadn't solved many of its prewar problems... For all its postwar Opportunity Plans and Redevelopment Acts, Chicago had little to show." It would've been reasonable to assume that the city's fortunes would continue to decline, the old boom-town vibrancy permanently moribund. Yet there were also signs of a coming revival, both cultural and economic: Mies van der Rohe had arrived before the war to take over the architectural department at IIT; Simone de Beauvoir was flying into town to spend time in a West Side walkup with Nelson Algren, not far from where Roger was born; its freight yards continued to process immense volumes of livestock, steel, and mail-order goods. For a young man like Roger, Chicago was still a space of possibility.

THE BEGINNING

Roger's demurrals notwithstanding, one could overstate reliance on luck. As Andrew advised, "A lot of his luck has come from hard work and preparedness and intelligence and empathy"—which is to say, it wasn't luck at all. Yet, Roger had the good fortune to be born into a well-connected family. And he took advantage of those connections. On a cruise in the late '40s or early '50s, Isidore and Gladys met Lester C. Roth, a senior partner and shareholder at the firm A.G. Becker. Upon learning that their son was fresh out of business school and looking for a job, Roth suggested that he come in for an interview.

By then, the company had a long history in Chicago. It had begun as Herbert Schaffner and Co., specializing in "commercial paper"—short term debts that companies assumed to cover payroll and other expenses. In 1893, Abraham G. Becker, then a junior partner at the company, bought out his boss for $50,000. The company grew under his watch into one of the country's leading producers of commercial paper.

Roger took the interview, then accepted a job at Becker without a clear sense of the future: "I didn't know what the hell the job was. Well, the job was to be a salesman." The position did not require a graduate degree from Harvard; as he remembered, "They were hiring guys out of high school to be salesmen—what the hell? But I didn't have any other things coming up, so I took it. I was a junior salesman." Roger was just the second salesman hired since the war. Despite Becker's reputation as an experienced, sophisticated firm, its training program was rudimentary: "They were totally incompetent in training salesmen," Roger recalls: "The sales manager didn't know what to do himself—how was he supposed to train me to be a salesman? Well, he didn't. So, I just screwed around a lot."

Investment banking was not a prestigious field then. Reflecting on his father's early career, Andrew admitted, "For him to go into investment banking and investment management was—I don't really have a sense that that was perceived as necessarily an interesting or coveted or prototypical career move in 1949-1950. But he really took to it pretty well." Before Roger could take to the work, though, he had to endure a purgatorial waiting period. "Before you could deal with the public, if you were a member of a New York Stock Exchange firm," Roger explained, "You had to pass a test and you had to work for six months, which I did." After he passed, Roger began making sales calls, using a stack of notecards with the information for prospects typed on them. His first sale was 10 shares of Ashland Oil to a female client. "She didn't know what she was doing but she had some money," Roger recalled. "I don't know if the sale worked out well or not. I think it did. It made me feel good."

Roger could've continued indefinitely making small sales for small dollars. Once again, geographical contingency intervened. Since his trip to Idaho in the 1930s, Roger had remained passionate about skiing, following the developments in the newborn sport, buying the latest gear. In the winters, he would fly to Denver and drive into the mountains. Denver was a smaller market than Chicago, but there were a few banks and mutual funds; some of them were Becker clients. But the salesman covering the region was not up to Roger's standards: "He wasn't doing anything, and he wasn't a very good

WORKING THE PHONES

Roger at A.G. Becker

salesman." Roger stepped in and got what he calls "good quality orders, thousands of shares to do this and that and the other." This was a turning point in Roger's career. Until that point, he had been making $300 a month; not an insignificant sum but not impressive, either; "slightly below the average of my classmates," in his accounting: "then when I started hitting it off in Denver and getting big orders, that made me rich. That was the beginning."

Roger's success in Denver caught the attention of the leadership at A.G. Becker. He was made Assistant Sales Manager, tasked with hiring, training, and retaining new salesmen. This was a challenge: most of the men—they were all men—whom Roger hired knew little about sales, and were ill-equipped for their new position. Reflecting on those years, Roger detailed the difficulties of the business for Becker's new hires:

> Selling securities is very tough. You have to deal with rich people, and you don't know rich people. And it's not only rich people; it's rich people who want to make investment decisions, or want to buy and sell stocks. So, they hired a lot of these guys that were out of college or the equivalent. They hadn't had experience as salespeople. It was my job to keep them floating for a while.

As Paul Judy, president and CEO of A.G. Becker during the 1970s, noted, Roger was careful about hiring his salesmen: "He had really thought through that function. He'd been a salesman himself, and he knew what should be the qualities and the profiles of the young people to bring in. And it wasn't necessarily what had been traditional in the field. He put a lot of emphasis on basic character, basic education, integrity, honesty, and a little more of an investment management function of feeling a responsibility, client responsibility." In a letter from the 1980s, advising his sons on their own careers, Roger himself echoed Judy,

> *Somehow your skills will be utilized—but they will be your basic skills—those that deal with understanding human nature and the culture in which you are working. Most of the specific technical skills you have accumulated will begin to atrophy as their need is diminished, though they will remain in your deep memory to be recalled and polished for action if and when the time comes.*

Recalling his protégés at A.G. Becker, Roger was modest: "Some of them turned out to be relatively successful. Not for what I did, but what they did by themselves." This is an understatement. Donald Rumsfeld worked for Roger. So did the billionaire investor and philanthropist Richard Gilder. Richard Elden, an analyst for Becker in the 1960s, created the first hedge funds in the United States; Barry Friedberg became the head of Investment Banking at Merrill Lynch. Many of these future luminaries remained close with Roger, regarding him as a mentor and friend. Members of the sales team at Becker would celebrate holidays with the Brown Family. John Rogers, a sales manager at Becker in the early 1970s, celebrated the fourth of July with the Browns at Northmoor Country

BOARD OF DIRECTORS MEETING
Circa 1968
Seated: Roger, Jim Lewis, Dave Dattelbaum,
Harry Weber, James Becker, Irv Sherman,
Bill Mabie, Ken Nelson
Standing: Mac Skall, Steve Weiss, Dave Heller,
Bill Cockrum, Burt Weiss, Jack Connor, Al Kopin,
John Mabie, Paul Judy

Club in 1973: Roger recounts in a letter from the time that the Brown and Rogers children enjoyed cotton candy, pony rides, and train rides together; they feasted on potato salad, coleslaw, fried chicken and hotdogs. These connections continued long after Roger had left Becker. In a letter from 1997, he casually mentioned having lunch with Rumsfeld, by then a former congressman, key advisor to Nixon and Ford, CEO of Searle, General Instrument, and chairman of Gilead Sciences.

Not all of Roger's hires went on to such distinguished careers. As Paul Judy remembered, one of the company's employees, John Pogue,

> *got into dealing with some really wild guys in a firm. They began to manipulate the shares and so on. And so before we knew it, Roger and I were heavily dealing with the SEC about John Pogue. We got through that process together. It took us two or three years. Roger was very central, and he took his responsibility seriously, but I never felt that he was really responsible for Pogue. I don't know who was. But I felt we, as an organization, somehow had brought in John Pogue, and he was a bad egg.*

Pogue was an anomaly in the corporate culture at Becker in the 1950s and 1960s. The environment in those early years was collaborative and collegial, with a free circulation of ideas. Roger described his team with pride: "Becker was probably the best sales group or the best brokerage firm in Chicago, besides Merrill Lynch. We got some real good guys and that made the difference."

As Roger was building his sales team, his immediate supervisor, Harry McCosh, died. Roger took his place. This was a rocky transition, particularly with A.G. Becker's New York office: "When the people found out in New York that I was going to be the boss of their boss, they didn't like it. They had a guy named Jim Lewis who was the local manager, and frankly he was a much better sales manager than I was, and I couldn't help him much. Also, whenever I appeared there, they wondered what the hell I was doing." Eventually, the management of the sales teams was split; Roger took the Chicago office and Jim Lewis took New York.

JIMMY BECKER

As he mentored future leaders, Roger himself was mentored by James Becker. "It's very hard to overstate how important James was to Roger," Andrew affirmed. During a wilderness trip with Outward Bound in the mid-1970s, Roger wrote a list of "10 people who have been influential, supportive and formative" in his life; "J.H. Becker" was fifth, behind "father; wife; mother; brother." The son of Abraham Becker, James was born in 1894, a year after his father bought the business. He joined the firm in 1921, after two years as a Lieutenant in the Army, fighting in World War I, and two years as the European director of the American Relief Administration. He spent the rest of his career at A.G. Becker and worked in all its offices. More than anyone else, he was responsible for transforming the firm from a respectable commercial paper business with a hundred-odd employees into a sophisticated financial concern with a thousand employees across the country. He became president of the company shortly before Roger arrived, in 1946.

In conversation, Roger could be reticent to describe precisely how James Becker shaped his career. "I don't think Jim actually taught me much as a sales manager might. But he was a very respected guy and extremely kind and gentle." Finally, Roger conceded, "Maybe I tried to behave like him once in a while." Andrew was more forthcoming:

> *He's got a photo portrait of Jimmy Becker that he's had in his office either at home or at work for decades. Because Jimmy meant that much to him. He was very meaningful in shaping how Roger thought about business and how he thought about integrity and how he thought about how to treat people and how the investment business had to work.*

FUNDS EVALUATION SERVICE

In the mid-1950s, John Mabie arrived at A.G. Becker. Though Mabie went on to found Mid-Continent Capital, he is not a household name like Donald Rumsfeld—nor is he a billionaire like Dick Gilder. Yet his influence on Roger's career is greater: the two worked as a team throughout much of Roger's time at A.G. Becker. Together, they developed an innovative and profitable financial instrument, which helped launch Roger into the firmament of Chicago business executives.

JIMMY BECKER

One of Roger's foremost mentors at A.G. Becker

John's dad was one of the firm's chief partners and later its president. Despite his father's prominence, John started working for Roger as a broker and salesman. His brother Jim also joined the firm around the same time. A recent graduate of Williams College, John was driven and inventive; Roger described him as a "very talented, bright guy." The Mabies were unusual at the firm: they were Gentiles in a company largely run by Jews. As Andrew described it, A.G. Becker resembled a Midwest Goldman Sachs: "They weren't exclusively hiring or promoting Jews, but it was *the* Jewish firm."

John worked, initially, with corporate officers. He observed that they often had huge assets in their retirement funds. These funds were bigger than the net worth of the companies themselves. But, as John remarked, "These guys have these pension funds and profit-share funds, and they don't know what the hell they're doing." There were no benchmarks to evaluate the success of their investments; no way to measure them against competing funds. Managers were doing the best they could, but they were losing money. Mabie wanted a way to evaluate the investments against similarly sized funds: "For that service we would get the commissions on their trades…with the banks and investment counselors that were managing the money." John and Roger started a service to evaluate such funds in 1965. By 1973, the year Roger left Becker, it accounted for 25% of the company's business. In dollar amounts, the funds evaluation service represented over half of what the firm's business had been in 1965.

"Well, funds evaluation was a brilliant idea. It was well-conceived, and it was profitable after it got going,"

Roger summarized. However, Mabie conceded in an interview, it was not immediately successful:

> We had to staff up for about four to five years and we lost money all the time because our expenses growing the business during this period of time. Becker wasn't making tremendous amounts of money and the service came under pressure now and then from the board. And Roger was steadfast in that it was a good idea. "We have the right people," he said; it was going to work. And then of course he was right and once it started to work, then the revenue flowed in on a regular basis. And we started doing business with all the major companies in the United States, and it was a very good business.

Vindicated in his defense of the funds evaluation service, Roger vaulted to the top of the company. He had been a member of the board since 1961; in 1966, he became a member of the executive committee; in 1968, he was elected senior vice president and vice chairman of the executive committee.

The success of the funds evaluation service was not enough, however, to salvage the fortunes of A.G. Becker. In the early 1970s, the company began to decline. This was partly due to competition. Big banks began imitating Roger and John. Competition drove down the price of the service and, as a result, Becker's margins. What began as an innovative and risky business quickly became a standard service. As Mabie conceded, "So then it became a more difficult business...it was about this time that A.G.

Becker began to sort of fall apart or however you want to call it. And the people who worked in that division, a lot of them went to Merrill Lynch."

But there were larger forces at work. The post-war boom was ending; over-production was rampant. Becker could no longer raise the capital it needed. Andrew explained the firm's difficulties:

> *Becker was a preeminent firm but at the end of the day...they needed "heightened additional capital" and their ability to get that was constrained by the nature of the time, which ended up leading to Becker's demise, leading to them being bought by two large European firms: Warburg and Paribas. British and French. That was clearly an element of why my dad said, "I can't get anything more done here. I don't have enough influence to control my own destiny with what's going to happen, as much as I have been able to."*

By 1973, Roger had enough and decided to leave Becker. In a letter written during a nine-hour planning meeting in the fall of 1973, he complained, "Next year as the firm goes through its planning process, I'll be doing something else. I have been through this process for over seven years. It is long and tiring and has become quite boring, but unfortunately necessary."

By the time Roger retired from Becker, he was a respected figure in Chicago business. He was chosen to represent Becker on the board of the Chicago Board Options Exchange (CBOE) when it was founded in 1973.

However eminent his position then, many of Roger's most profitable and prestigious accomplishments were still to come. He reflected:

> *When I look back at these early years, they are so far away from the financial success that our family has achieved, that I have difficulty determining what the important ingredients were that fueled this accumulation. The thought that recurs during this activity is the pleasant enjoyment my father would have in knowing that his two sons have accomplished so much. But I shouldn't forget that we had a running start, coming from a well to do upper middle class family and having benefitted by attending elite educational institutions, and not being burdened by student loans.*

The seeds of Roger's wealth were planted during his tenure at Becker. He had been asked to become a stockholder, a privilege "comparable to being invited into an exclusive partnership." As Roger recalled, "When people at Becker were made stockholders, it had the same aura of becoming partners. It was recognition and a promotion without a change in compensation with the opportunity to invest and participate in the firm's profits and losses." These proved to be excellent investments. Moreover, Roger dutifully saved every year, money from his own salary and money he received as gifts and loans from his parents. Together, these investments formed the foundation of his fortune. "In effect," Roger recounted, "I was on my way to becoming rich."

JUST BEFORE NEW YORK

May 22 1954, Howard's Room

Isidore, Howard, & Roger before Howard traveled
to New York

READY FOR A FORMAL EVENT

Mid 1960s

Roger & Barbara

Chapter 3
FROM FAIREST CREATURES

EARLY IN HIS CAREER AT A.G. BECKER, Roger offered investment advice to Min Russell, *née* Schoenberg, a casual acquaintance from Chicago. According to Roger, she was looking for "the simplest investment advice: should she buy Peoples Gas or not?" She was evidently impressed by the young investment manager: "She liked me. I think financial safety was very important to her, so she introduced me to her daughter Barbara." Roger ascribed this meeting to chance, once again working in his favor. The chance meeting yielded long term dividends—likely longer than Roger's investment advice to Min Russell: "I don't know if Barbara would admit this, but she chased the hell out of me, and she caught me, and I was very lucky."

Louis Mann, the rabbi at Chicago Sinai Temple, wedded Barbara and Roger in his study on May 16, 1953, followed by a small family dinner. Like his parents, Roger stayed close to home for his honeymoon: the newlyweds celebrated at the Hotel Moraine on the shore of Lake Michigan in Highland Park. The hotel has been shuttered since 2006, but at the time, it was a glamorous vacation spot. Roger was unimpressed: "Well, that was adequate. I wouldn't advise anybody to go there for their honeymoon, but it was satisfactory for us."

Roger detected a reticence between Barbara and his parents early in the relationship, resulting from the families' different fortunes: "She was not in the same social class as I was. And so, I think Isidore was very careful about what he said or did, initially." Her family were

ABE & MIMI

Barbara's mother Min with Abe Cohen, her second husband. They married in 1960 and shared many happy years. Their apartment was home to many weekend sleepovers, not only for Roger and Barbara's children, but Howard and Betsy's girls as well.

Romanian and Russian Jewish émigrés; Barbara grew up worshipping at an orthodox temple in Chicago. But her family hadn't had the Brown's good fortune. Barbara's father, Seymour, died just before the start of World War II from lingering complications of a gas attack in World War I. Barbara, perhaps 12 at the time, was called on to help the family. As her grandson Joey recalled, "her older brother Maynard was not a particularly willing and helping hand, so Barbara had to do a lot of housework at a younger age to support her family. She cooked plenty of meals!" Owen described her initial efforts in the kitchen: "Apparently the first few meals didn't go quite as planned. Mom told us that she always had her nose in a book, which resulted in the burning of more than one dish."

Barbara's mother worked as a milliner. She was a skilled seamstress and by the time she was about 16, she was out-earning her father, Sam Schoenberg, a Romanian immigrant who worked as a house painter. After her husband died, Min returned to work, eventually purchasing a store across Marshall Field's, selling women's hats.

In her spare time, Barbara enjoyed going to the branch library (her "second home") in Austin, the West Side neighborhood where the family lived, as well as watching Shirley Temple movies. She spent her summers on her uncle Sidney's farm in Wisconsin. She earned a bachelor's degree in economics from the University of Illinois. However, as Roger recounted, the family's fortunes remained precarious and eventually suffered another reversal: "Min struggled for years, and put two children through college by designing women's hats, and then they went out of style." Despite the class difference between Barbara's family and her new husband's, they soon warmed to each other; Isidore gifted Barbara her first pair of birdwatching binoculars.

Nearly a decade passed after Barbara and Roger's marriage before Howard joined his brother among the ranks of married men, wedding Betsy Kassel in 1962. By then, Howard was 35. He had served as a foreign correspondent and purchased the *Kenosha News*. But he remained a bachelor until meeting Betsy in Middletown, New York. Betsy remembered how delighted Roger, Barbara, Isidore, and Gladys were "that Howard was finally going to get married because he was 35 years old, and they liked me. They wondered what kind of—he had many girlfriends, but I was the only one apparently who... I don't know, I was the one he settled on, so they were just absolutely thrilled about our marriage." Betsy recalled, "We were close to them...as family." Besides gathering on holidays, they traveled together regularly, and Roger served on the board of the *Kenosha News*.

HIGHLAND PARK PETTING ZOO

Roger and Barbara moved around in the early years of their marriage: from an apartment in Chicago to another in Evanston, where their first two children, Jeffrey and Owen were born. In 1956, they settled on ten acres of orchard, wood, and marshland in the then mostly undeveloped suburb of Highland Park, Illinois. Roger had strict criteria when the couple was shopping for homes:

CHRISTMAS
1954
Roger with Jeffrey

JUST BEFORE THE WEDDING
May 15 1953, Isidore & Gladys' library
1335 Astor St.
Barbara, Roger, & Min

I told her I wanted a house that has two stories, that is in walking distance to the train, that doesn't have any grounds to worry about, so on and so forth. Then we were looking, we were looking for weeks and months. We came across this house. It had none of those characteristics. We both looked at it, looked at it together, and we bought it. And we ended up redoing it, adding to it, monkeying with it for...well, we've been here for 60 years.

Seduced by its space and quiet, its orchard and gardens, the young couple overlooked some of the house's downsides, including its sagging floorboards. As the family settled in, the boisterous lives of children, and their many pets, beat back the suburban quiet. Roger's son Owen has described the house as a "petting zoo," a chaotic abundance of life. Roger remembered, "We often had dogs. A cat maybe... my wife had some birds. Then I think she might have had turtles there for the kids. And there were turtles in the creek." Owen corrected the record:

We always had dogs from 1957 onwards. And we had Callie the cat (as she was calico) who lost her leg in an auto accident at Thanksgiving, and then, thanks to Dad's quick work at taking her to the vet, became a 3-legged indoor cat. That was the last time she climbed onto a car engine block to stay warm!

One of the family's dogs, Pippi, would wander around the neighborhood, unsupervised; the Browns received angry phone calls from neighbors who found him, or excremental evidence of his presence, in their yards. The others—Hector, Wolf, Whiskers, Toby, Daisy, Spot, and Robbie—were less errant. Alongside these canine companions were parakeets, gerbils, mice, tadpoles, goldfish, to say nothing of the snakes who found their way down the chimney periodically. Barbara would also collect dead birds, put them in the freezer, and then bring them to the Field Museum for their collections.

A number of people came to work for the Browns in the house and became *de facto* parts of the household: for instance, Montrose Beard, a crane operator who also worked part time as a handyman. "Mr. Beard was a salt of the earth kind of person," Andrew remembered: "it was hard for the kids to gauge how old he was. He probably came three days a week and ate at the table with the Browns. He was very fond of Barbara and really part of the family." There was also domestic help: Myrtle Baldwin, who had helped Barbara's mother, and Elswith Belisle from Belize, a live-in maid with her own small room in the house. She worked 12-hour days, Tuesdays through Saturdays, helping Barbara with cleaning, cooking, and watching the children. She became so essential to the family that Roger and Barbara set up an annuity for her when she retired. Most importantly, Min stayed overnight to do the sewing and mending, for a few days every few weeks, even after she remarried in her sixties.

Once established in Highland Park, Roger and Barbara slowly expanded the house and fixed it up, widening the dining room, adding a porch (which became a conservatory), a den, two more children's bedrooms, two bathrooms, and the "new room," roughly doubling

BEHAVING THEMSELVES

September 1970 at 1261 Clavey Road

Owen, Andy, Henry, and Jeff

the square footage in the process. Owen remembered this construction as a constant presence in the family's life during the 1960s and early 1970s:

I can remember walking through these areas playing my flutophone, so I must have been in third grade, maybe 1963 or '64, and the studs were in place. You could smell the cut wood...Little by little they expanded the grounds around the home. Then 10 or 15 years ago, my mother decided that she was going to put a large grassy area back into native prairie, and so they added that as well. Even though it was my mother's impetus, I think my father really did strongly enjoy expanding the world of nature.

As the house expanded, the family grew with it. Roger and Barbara eventually had five children: Jeffrey and Owen, followed by Andrew, Henry, and Vanessa. They had another daughter, Elizabeth, in between Owen and Andrew who died suddenly in infancy. Roger remembered, "she died in what they call crib death, or sudden infant death syndrome. All of a sudden your daughter's dead. Barbara handled it amazingly well." Andrew, born a few years later, admired how both of his parents soldiered on, despite the heartbreak:

Honestly, I never remember that slowing them down or them even thinking about it. And it's not like they avoided it. You could ask my mom about it directly and she'd be like, "Well, this is who she was; this is what happened. It's unfortunate, but it happened."

She just shrugged it off, but I'm sure that it wasn't so easy at the time.

This may reflect the couple's pragmatic attitude toward tragedy and danger. Owen recalls that his parents considered building a fallout shelter in the 1960s; they even acquired plans for it: "And then Roger thought, 'Oh, why bother? We don't want to live in a world that's been atomic-bombed.' So they just went on without that investment."

INFINITE OPPORTUNITIES

Roger and Barbara's marriage settled along traditional lines. Roger went to work downtown; Barbara stayed home with the kids. Roger was the family disciplinarian; Barbara was a loving and nurturing matriarch. Owen and Jeffrey recall listening to her read Maurice Maeterlinck's *The Blue Bird* aloud on the couch. As Jeffrey wrote, years later, recalling the experience, "What [mattered] was that for an hour or so, during a quiet time in the afternoon, Owen and I would spend some intimate time listening to our mother read one of her favorite childhood books to us." She cared not only for her own children but Howard's as well, fielding phone calls from the girls during moments of crisis. Roger's niece Amy remembered: "I've called Barbara up to say, 'Something's wrong with the chicken I baked. My mom's not home,' or 'How can I tell when the turkey's done?'"

Despite her misadventures in the kitchen as a girl, Barbara loved food and she became a good cook. She hosted the big holidays at home: Thanksgiving, New Year's Day, Passover, Mother's Day, Father's Day. "Barbara was an amazing hostess," Lucy noted, "She always seemed to so effortlessly put on just such a splendid meal." She was famous for her homemade cheesecakes served at New Year's parties and for her spaghetti; her chocolate torte and her cookies were among the family's favorite treats. She kept an organized kitchen, with specific serving dishes for specific meals: two or three aluminum serving dishes for vegetables and a green ceramic dish with a heavy lid for Kraft macaroni and cheese.

Vegetables and fruit from her backyard garden and orchard supplemented the family's diet, including cherries that she froze to use later in pies. Henry remembers "a couple of years where there were really big harvests of cherries. And this is not really a Roger thing, but we'd have these big operations where we'd be pitting all these cherries to freeze." Roger carved meat for meals; the Brown kids joined Barbara in the kitchen, learning to cook by experimenting with new dishes, sometimes unintentionally. During a dinner at Howard's, Betsy accidentally burned the chicken—badly. Henry dug in. After a few bites, he looked up from his plate, thoughtfully chewing his food, and announced, "Aunt Betsy, this is the best burnt chicken I've ever had!" It became one of her delicacies in succeeding years.

At Passover, Barbara gathered walnut, *matzos*, wine, bitter herbs, and gefilte fish. She usually worked without a recipe, assembling her haroset (and on Chanukah, her latkes) from instinct and experience. The *haggadahs*, Maxwell House version, were stored in the attic. Henry was often delegated to retrieve them in later years: Owen speculated that he was assigned the task because "of his education as a medical student, it was thought he wouldn't hurt himself, or perhaps because he was the nearest at hand at the request."

On these occasions, Howard and his wife Betsy drove down from Kenosha with their children; Isidore and Gladys would drive up from Chicago. "I truly enjoy every minute of it," Roger wrote to the family in 1973: "The women talking and working in the kitchen...The hunt for the *afikomen* with little children racing around the house laughing and screaming; the reading of the *haggadah* with everyone participating in a self-conscious way. The prayers over the wine." Howard served as banker for the night, with a silver dollar for the finder of the *afikomen*. In a letter from April 1974, Roger described Vanessa, then in kindergarten, discovering it: "Her uncle Maynard hid it under one of the corners of the living room carpet... You can't imagine the elation and excitement that Vanessa showed. It was as though a bolt of lightning had shot through her as she screamed and jumped into the dining room among the shrieks of her brother and cousins and the accolades of her parents, grandparents, aunts, and uncles." At the end of the night, Gladys would speak. As Lucy recollected:

> *When Gladys wanted to speak, there was always a moment of silence. And Grandma was going to get up and say a poem to commemorate the occasion. And it was often something that she found, I think, in a Hallmark card. And Poppy would take a*

A RECEPTION FOR HOWARD & BETSY
March 2 1960
Seated: Isidore & Gladys, Muriel & Murray Kassel
Standing: Roger & Barbara, Betsy & Howard

spoon, and he would knock on the glassware to get everybody's attention. And my God, you had better not be talking. You had better not be talking. There had to be complete silence.

Such solemnity aside, the atmosphere of these family gatherings was relaxed and spontaneous. Yet they also occasioned deeper reflections on the family's good fortune and place in the world. In 1974, Roger wrote the family:

Thanksgiving and Pesach are my two favorite holidays. I like them both because they bring the whole family together and take substantial effort to prepare and serve...As opposed to most other holidays, there is no exchange of gifts or special symbolism (other than during the meal)—these are both spiritual holidays thanking God for life as free people. Each of us has been so fortunate that it is fitting that an opportunity such as these holidays permits us to realize our own good fortune and revel in our happiness. We have these benefits not merely because we have accumulated extra wealth but because we are physically healthy and mentally gifted and alert. More important, we are not slaves unto Pharaoh, nor are we living in fear about our next meal as are millions in Africa, Asia, and South America. The opportunities for each of us to improve ourselves and build values into the future are infinite.

BAWDY JOKES AND BIRDWATCHING

Despite the traditional contours of her marriage, Barbara herself was hardly a stereotypical "housewife." Henry, for instance, invoked her "surprisingly bawdy sense of humor." Her parenting was infused with spontaneity, even when her children were misbehaving. In elementary school, Andrew had as his teacher a stern southern belle with a pronounced limp, the result of a recent surgery: "She looked like a female version of the classic cartoon character, Foghorn Leghorn, the pompous southern rooster. I couldn't help burst out laughing at her." The teacher called Barbara to complain; the offending child trudged home with "a lot of trepidation." Barbara met him at the back door and launched into a stern lecture. "I looked up and told her that I couldn't help it, the situation was too funny. At that, we both burst out laughing."

She was just as willing to laugh at her own foibles and missteps. She often recounted the first dinner party she gave after her marriage. She had prepared sweetbreads—but a friend gently intervened, suggesting she consider an alternate entrée in case some of her guests didn't like them. Searching for an alternate dish, she settled on liver: she loved chicken and turkey livers. Unfortunately, her guests didn't share her enthusiasm: none of them would touch it.

Though Barbara had studied economics in college, her passion was for science; she'd even considered majoring in biology. As Owen noted, "Mom majored in econ because she could get a job with that degree; she couldn't as a biologist, or so she thought." In the late 1960s, she returned to her early passion as a volunteer in the

Department of Mammals at Chicago's Field Museum, where she worked for Phil Hershkovitz, a mammologist specializing in the mammals of South America. After a few weeks on the job, she realized why there had been an opening for her position: Hershkovitz couldn't keep an assistant for more than a month. His standards were exacting; he'd fire people for the most minor mistakes. Barbara matched Hershkovitz's demands with her own attention to detail, eventually becoming a trusted assistant, closely attached to the mammalogy program at the Museum. She did fieldwork with him in the Cerrado savanna and the coastal forests in Brazil, baiting and trapping animals. After Hershkovitz retired, she worked for Lawrence Heaney, a mammologist who specialized in the mammals of the Philippines.

There are several species named after Barbara: a nocturnal climbing rodent from Peru (*Isothrix barbarabrownae*), a Brazilian monkey (*Callicebus barbarabrownae*), known as the blond titi, a mouse in the Philippines (*Apomys brownorum*), and a prehistoric bird (*Vadaravis brownae*). The blond titi was believed extinct in the early 1990s; living members of the species were rediscovered in 1997 in the coastal highlands of Brazil's Bahia and Sergipe states. Those names indicate the respect she enjoyed among the research staff at the Field Museum. She was appointed as an honorary associate in the Division of Mammals in 1990, "in recognition of [her] dedicated work, and generous contributions to Field Museum and the Division of Mammals," as the Museum's then vice-president, Jonathan Hass wrote. She continued working there two days a week into her 80s.

Yet Barbara's deepest passion was not for mammals but birds. She told her granddaughter Ariana, "I hope that when I die, I'll be in heaven with those who taught me how to do birdwatching." She and her friends Margot Merrick and Patty Ware went on regular birdwatching trips to the Chicago Botanic Gardens. Several of her sons have followed in Barbara's footsteps and become dedicated birdwatchers. Roger did not share this passion, despite Barbara's best efforts. On a journey to Florida in 1973, for instance, they visited Corkscrew Swamp, a national wildlife preserve. At the time, Roger was optimistic about his future as an amateur ornithologist, writing to the family: "Mom is getting me over the edge toward becoming a bird watcher."

The enthusiasm was passing. Years later, Roger confessed, "I never got going on birdwatching. I feel so stupid, I can't identify very ordinary birds now." Instead, he was drawn to human accomplishments. As he wrote during his 1975 Outward Bound trip, "I am not an outdoorsman and after this trip I doubt if my interest in camping or hiking or natural scenic beauty will increase. I am more impressed by the aspects of life which are the creation of human input to modern civilization."

Barbara loved nature and was a committed conservationist, a passion sparked by her reading of Rachel Carson's 1962 book *Silent Spring*. But she was not sentimental or idealistic about the natural world. When her grandsons Aaron and Joey were teenagers, they asked Roger and Barbara to take them to Walden Pond.

Joey recalled:

> *I still remember Barbara saying something like, "Thoreau was an excessively boring writer," which when you're like 13 and 14, you're reading things like "Civil Disobedience" and "A Plea for Captain John Brown." You're so enamored...and I don't know, maybe I was also going camping a lot more back then, so you read these things, kind of think about, I don't know, just sitting out in the woods and planting your bean rows...and Barbara, despite being a person really invested in the natural world, just found these things kind of frivolous and stupid.*

Joey doesn't remember Roger objecting to Barbara's judgment, though Roger too went through a youthful infatuation with the transcendental hermit. In a letter from 1947, Roger offers Thoreau as a model of the life he would've liked to lead: "Thoreau was himself; he merely sustained himself so that he was able to live as he wished."

Roger and Barbara's marriage was not without complications. Amy remembered Barbara issuing a warning: "Be careful if you marry a wolf. A wolf will never be home and will always be demanding, and it's not easy." Amy elaborated the moral of Barbara's lupine allegory: "Then there you go, that was Roger. It's hard to marry a very successful, ambitious person and anticipate that he's going to be Mr. Rogers, you know?" Whatever the tensions provoked by Roger's personality, he and Barbara mostly lived in harmony. They shared an intellectual life, reading and discussing the same books, though she read faster than Roger and devoured mystery novels prodigiously.

Their politics sometimes aligned: Barbara had worked for the Cook County Democratic Party as a young woman, an experience of waste, incompetence, and corruption so horrifying it made her a life-long Republican. They went to Ravinia and the opera together. Hannah, one of Barbara's granddaughters, asked her what she liked about Roger: "and she goes, 'He was handsome,' and then she paused, and she goes, 'Both physically and intellectually.'"

Their marriage embodied the opposite of the Thoreauvian ideal, as Roger stated it above: rather than an ecstatic independence, their sixty-year companionship was grounded in mutuality and compromise, even where their interests diverged. On the eve of Valentine's Day, and Barbara's birthday in 1986, Roger wrote to the family:

> *How fortunate each of you are to have a relationship with this fine, loving, bright and energetic woman. For some of us, she is a pushy Jewish Mama, for others a caring daughter, and for me, a wonderful, loving companion full of wisdom, common sense, information—and she's a good cook too. The years come and go, but ours just seem to keep flowing on as if they'll continue forever. How pleasant.*

GOOD, BUT IS IT ENOUGH?

Highland Park became for Roger a refuge from business. He enjoyed eating breakfast with family members gathered around the table and WFMT playing classical music in the background. Each evening after work, he would do a calisthenic routine adapted from a booklet published by the Royal Canadian Air Force. Henry noted, "He also used to regularly jog the 1.5 miles around the subdivision to the south of us. This was in the 60s and 70s, long before running became a popular form of exercise." At dinner, he would join Barbara and the children. Andrew observed:

> *She was very focused on proper manners at the table, which we mostly ignored, but she would kind of discipline unruly kids and expected Roger to help her with that, which he did. It was a real dinner, a three-course dinner every night. Salad or soup, always a main course with a side, and always a dessert. Every night.*

Then Roger retreated to his den to finish the day's work, coming out only when Barbara, the first line of defense, needed reinforcement disciplining the children. Roger and Barbara generally trusted their children and allowed them some latitude. The children had checking accounts in their early teens, which they balanced each month; they also made arrangements on their own to fly back and forth to Exeter. For Andrew, "that was a cause for some anxiety when I was a thirteen-year-old, especially when Owen told me 'get tickets for us both to make sure we're on the same plane,' and I didn't have enough in my account to pay for two round-trip tickets. That was a problem."

YOUNG PARENTS

March 20 1954

Roger & Barbara with their firstborn, Jeff

Yet Barbara and Roger's parenting was not entirely *laissez-faire*. Traditions, small and large, were important in the Brown household, checking their children's independence. As Roger wrote to Owen when he turned 18,

> *Unfortunately, it is easier to govern by rules instead of judgment—precedence is more important than reason, and tradition still continues, though weakened by the continuous onslaught of liberalism. The loss of many of these traditions has created great freedom, but with this liberalization it has brought on greater levels of crime, disrespect for duty and honor. Reverence is becoming an obsolescent word. So all isn't bright and good and improving bit by bit everyday—the devil still lives and co-exists with truth and peace. Being 18 doesn't mean that you are to devote your life to fighting the devil—but neither is it license to ignore tradition nor to renege on your duty.*

Not all Brown traditions were so existential. When Howard and Roger were children, Isidore and Gladys took them downtown each Christmas to see Marshall Field's Christmas windows on State Street; the brothers did the same with their children.

Again, Roger followed Isidore and Gladys' example and sent his children to Exeter. When his grandchildren came of age, he encouraged them to follow in their footsteps. In 1985, upon Vanessa's graduation from Exeter, he wrote to the family, "This event will mean that our contacts with the school will be much less frequent and little by little we will depend on grandchildren to matriculate there so that we may be able to reacquaint ourselves with the lovely campus and the spirit of the school." As Hannah recounted, "He was always mad that my brothers and I didn't go to Exeter. He and Barbara would bring it up all the time: '*Why* didn't you go?'"

While preserving tradition, Roger could still be responsive to the needs of individual children. Andrew did not thrive at Exeter, and eventually finished high school at North Shore Country Day. In his letters, Roger treated the crisis as a teachable moment:

> *Flunking out of Exeter is not a sin nor is it a permanent set-back from which one cannot recover. Therefore, if the worst occurs, your life will go on and so will ours. However, we do know that you are a rather competitive, goal-oriented person and that under normal circumstances you will do what is necessary to succeed. We therefore anticipate that your mid-term performance will act merely as an incentive to more thoughtful and more thorough work that will permit you to achieve those goals to which you aspire.*

Andrew went on to receive three degrees from the University of Chicago and is now a successful real estate developer, and a principal at Kinzie Realty. Roger thought his "number three son, Andrew, is the closest to me in terms of things he was good at and stuff of that nature." Despite their shared interests, Roger and Andrew rarely discussed business in any detail. "Not that he wasn't available for advice should I want it or look for it," Andrew explained, "but I'd have to ask for it rather than him poke his nose into my business. I think he really felt that it was in many ways better to find my own way."

But not all of Roger's children flourished in his household. Roger's youngest child, Vanessa, noted, "I love my dad very much, but it's a hard relationship. He has so many strengths, he's unbelievably intelligent, but I think due to when he was raised and how he was raised, he is not in tune with his emotions or other people's emotions or very sensitive. He's a horrible teaser." Betsy concurred, "Roger was always a bit of a tease; sometimes that didn't go over too well: people could resent it. Vanessa used to love to come to our house because she found it so much warmer." Roger's own writings betray little of this tension. Instead, his letters tend to recount moments of shared joy, like a cross country skiing expedition on the grounds of Northmoor Country Club in the winter of 1974:

> *Mom & Vanessa came along. Vanessa's boots and skis had Alpine bindings and stiff boots so it didn't take long for her to skin her heel. This meant that Mom & Dad had to pull her without poles. Wolf frolicked along with us, attacking the tip of each ski as it moved forward. Luckily, she stayed far enough away from our poles so that we didn't end up with skewered terrier for dinner.*

With Roger's sons away at school in the early 1970s, he began writing a weekly letter—first to them, later

VANESSA WITH BARBARA & ROGER

November 1985

to the family as a whole. The letters form a record of events both historic and mundane: Vanessa losing—and swallowing—a tooth, with much ado for the tooth fairy; Owen getting into Yale; the end of the Vietnam War; the dismissal of Archibald Cox. Roger typically wrote the letters longhand in a single draft, without revision; a secretary would then transcribe them. Roger encouraged his children to reciprocate his letters and thereby develop a personal literary style. He could be an exacting tutor in this regard. When Henry was at camp, for instance, Roger chided him: "We are looking forward to getting some letters from you, and other than those scribbly little things you used to write in the last couple of years, we would like to have you spend a little effort improving your style and learning to expostulate." This emphasis on style descended from Isidore: as Roger wrote, describing his father's prose:

> He is a great stylist and writes imaginatively weaving in quotations from great writers of the past. This is a style that is fast disappearing as youngsters of my generation and yours too were not forced and encouraged to memorize drama and poetry. This is unfortunate as the suffering of learning more than compensates for the later pleasures of utilizing these skills. I know that I get some enjoyment from my ability to recite a few lines of Chaucer—something of negligible value, but practically the only thing I had to memorize since the Boy Scout's Oath.

Despite the pride Roger took in his letters, and the attention he paid over the years to their composition, he did not reread them. In a letter from 1989, he explained why:

> *I am afraid to read them for a combination of reasons. Most threatening is the fear of boredom. The second concern is the long list of pessimistic predictions which proved to be wrong—at least so far. Then lastly in reviewing them may come the realization that I have had a "successful" yet empty life. How unfortunate or how honest I must be even to write such words. I think I have accomplished what most people or living creatures do—raise a family—but that's standard for continuing existence. What successes I have had can be looked at in retrospect as reflecting my cultural background and my parents' desires and ambitions. I have fit into the standards of expectations but not much more. That's good but is it enough?*

ISIDORE VISITING
July 1965, 1261 Clavey Road
*Isidore, Barbara, Roger, & the seldom-used
basketball hoop*

OPENING NIGHT AT THE LYRIC OPERA
October 12 1962
Howard & Betsy, Isidore & Gladys, Roger & Barbara
see Borodin's Prince Igor

RECEPTION
1990
Roger & Barbara

Chapter 4
LUXURY AND THRIFT

IN THE FALL OF 1973, as he prepared to leave A.G. Becker, Roger wrote his sons to describe a lecture he had recently attended on the history of the Promised Land. The letter closes with a brief meditation: "History is a fascinating study and one that adds dimension to life and increases the breadth and depth of understanding of some of the apparent absurd things that are occurring in the world today."

In the midst of Watergate and the close of the Vietnam War, history likely did seem a chain of absurdities. Facing an unpredictable present, Roger characteristically turned to the past: he was not just a student of history; he absorbed and applied its lessons to his own life. Andrew argued that his father's sense of the past contributed to his success as an investor: "Part of the reason he was interested in the work is because academically, intellectually, he was really interested in history." For example, reading a biography of Aaron Burr in the fall of 1974, Roger wrote to the family,

> *I wish we had better insights about what the leading people worried and talked about during their many crises. I am certain we would find the bulk of their concerns similar to our own, except that now we talk of oil prices, food shortages and illiquidity of the monetary system; then they were concerned with land company swindles, government corruption and international intrigue with France, Spain and Britain right on our borders.*

Confronting a figure like Burr gave Roger the sense of *longue durée* necessary to endure the shocks of the moment. His approach to crisis—whether the interlocking crises of the early 1970s or the Black Monday market collapse in 1987—is clear-eyed, reflecting on the long-term trajectories of the market, not short-term spasms.

Yet even for Roger, the pace of events during the early 1970s may have been disorienting. In September 1974, Roger wrote to his sons: "I have been a bit battered lately by horrible economic news and the abysmally weak stock market. One would almost think that the world is coming to an end." In a letter from 1973, as he retired from A.G. Becker, he took a more philosophical angle:

> *Events throughout the world have been moving very fast in the last several months. The uncertainties that have been created and the suddenness of these events have brought to mind the title of a book published several years ago—Future Shock—the only difference now is that we are living in "present shock." Communications have accelerated and interpretation and analysis follow so quickly that no one has time or technique to think things out—they are just happening and blurring in front of him. All of this is further complicated by the interdependence of Western society. Though we may pollute the environment and be wasteful of our natural resources, our economy is extremely efficient...Occupations such as mine would be nonexistent if there was not a high level of commercial order. However, the more complex this order is, the*

*easier it is to disrupt. And now disruptions are and
will occur from almost any cause and direction. The
future skill will be to be totally prepared for these
disruptions prior to their occurrence.*

It was in this environment that Roger left A.G. Becker
for a brief period of unemployment, then founded his own
investment house. If this was a bold move in the midst of
such economic flux, it also reflected Roger's sense for a
good business opportunity. "Naturally, there are anxious
and uncertain moments whenever a change is made," he
wrote in the same letter, "but there is also opportunity
and excitement. I feel confident that such changes can
reinvigorate and stimulate development."

On a Wednesday in January 1974, the board of directors at A.G. Becker gave a farewell party for Roger and
Jack Connor at the Tavern Club in Chicago. The firm
presented Roger an engraved silver platter, a hand-illu-
minated and hand-printed book with a resolution by the
board in his honor, and a pair of skis. Isidore and Howard
were both in attendance. Unbeknownst to Roger, Howard
was the featured speaker. A copy of this speech has not
survived, but Roger was evidently moved by his brother's
tribute. "He was magnificent," Roger told the family, "It
was a wonderful event—one which I shall never forget."

BUILDING A SOLID BUSINESS

In a 1973 letter to his sons, Roger added, as an aside, "I have made arrangements to office with The Harris Group who are a group of men concentrating in the investment of funds for themselves and their clients... Initially my work will be on some private family affairs, but while officing there, I will be looking around to better determine if there are other things that I would like to do."

The Harris Group had been founded by Chicago businessman Irving Harris. He and his brother Neison Harris started the Toni Company together in 1946 to manufacture home hair permanents. Thanks in part to an iconic slogan—"Which Twin Has the Toni?"—the company became a household name. Neison served as the public face of the company; Irving worked behind the scenes analyzing investments and guiding the company's growth. In the 1950s, they sold the firm for $50 million.

Irving did not initially intend to create an investment management fund: he simply hired staff to help him invest and manage the money. As Peter Foreman recalls, Irving was heavily involved in a number of other businesses, including Standard Shares, where he was chairman. His little investment entity was no more than a distraction. It did some investment counseling, had a small and unprofitable fund, Acorn—managed from the start by Ralph Wanger. But it also had some promising pieces: Morningstar, a profitable options trading partnership on the CBOE, as well as a seat on the NYSE. His investment fund had grown into a business in its own right, more successful than Irving had hoped.

Roger recalled:

> *Irving decided, several times, that he wanted to get out of the business. And he didn't know how to do it simply, and he didn't want to fire the people that were around him. Because he had some very talented people that were working there. And so, he set up a deal where the employees could buy the business. And then, by the time he walked to the railroad station, he reneged. He did it twice.*

Finally, Harris found a compromise that suited him: he recruited Roger—already experienced in managing a large organization—to take over the business. The two had first met during Roger's tenure at Becker. According to Owen, "Roger met Harris when Harris hired A.G. Becker to sell his business to Gillette. An executive named D.B. Stern handled the deal. Jimmy Becker had Roger liaise with the Harrises because he didn't want to."

Roger did not respond immediately to Harris' overture. Instead, as Peter Foreman, one of the founding partners of Harris Associates recounted, Roger scrutinized the company:

> *So Roger, in his typical detailed fashion, over the next month or whatever, interviewed each of us with a pen and paper; had a whole list of questions for each of us; wrote down the answers. I don't remember all the questions, but there was a long list and a long interview before he decided to take this job on, and how he wanted to be involved with this.*

After completing his study, Roger said to himself, "Yeah, we have a business here that can survive and maybe grow. But Irving has to not renege." With Peter Foreman, Myron Szold, Vic Morgenstern, Ralph Wanger, and Joe Braucher, all of whom had been working for Irving or co-officing with him, Roger purchased the business from Harris for the book value of the furniture and fixtures: "We didn't pay him anything, any premium that he deserved. He should've gotten it. But I think he got tired of trying to sell it." Foreman, who brought in the most revenue of the six, and was most enthusiastic about Roger's involvement, initially took 25% of the partnership interest; Roger, the second largest share. They called their new business Harris Associates and opened their doors on the first day of the year, 1976.

The company's name came from Irving Harris. After selling the business, he continued to share offices with Harris Associates, albeit with a separate staff working for him. He was not financially or personally involved in the business. The relationship between Harris and the company named after him was not always easy. Owen was told it was "cordial." Roger elsewhere used slightly stronger terms. As he wrote in a letter from 2004, just after Harris' death:

> *I had a continuous period of business dealings with him, and though they were not pleasant, they were not acrimonious. I saved him from the problem of firing all the people who had worked with him...but never got a word of thanks, nor an acknowledgement of the success of our efforts in building a solid*

*business. Everything seemed to require a grudging
negotiation, even the naming of our business "Harris
Associates." We did this in an effort to maintain
whatever good will and clientele that we inherited.
Looking backwards, it was a reasonable mistake,
as he never honored us with any new business, but
benefited by the sharing of facilities. Though he had
nothing to do with our company, he frequently and
unknowingly got credit for our successes.*

Roger also described Harris with grudging respect,
acknowledging his business acumen and his philanthropy:
"Irving touched many lives through his generous and
public philanthropy."

In an interview, Peter Foreman speculated about
Roger's motivations in this period, why he chose to found
a new company so soon after his retirement from A.G.
Becker, in a period of economic turmoil: "Why did Roger
step forward to take over Harris Associates? I think he
saw a challenge, and he liked challenges, because he could
keep score with a challenge. On a challenge you're either
a winner or a loser."

THINK

At its founding, Harris Associates had around 15
employees, most of them holdovers from Irving Harris'
investment office. As Roxanne Martino, who would soon
be a key player in Harris Associates' success, reflected in
an interview, Roger faced challenges in managing them:
"Normally, it's five people and they say, 'Come on, let's

EARLY DAYS OF HARRIS ASSOCIATES

1979

Roger at an ADP or Quotron terminal

start a business.' They're all trying to row in the same direction. At the beginning, Roger didn't have that." Yet Roger held the team he had inherited from Irving Harris in high esteem:

> *He had some really bright guys. Among them was Ralph Wanger. And then, he had Peter Foreman, who had left Glore Forgan to work for Irving. And both of those guys were just a handful. They were really very, very talented. They could have gone to bigger firms; they didn't have any interest in that. I would guess Peter Foreman used to get an offer every couple of months. And Ralph Wanger was an acknowledged genius, but nobody wanted to hire him. He was a queer duck.*

As managing partner, Roger was responsible for the daily operations of the firm, including managing the big personalities in his office. His leadership style did not reflect a natural genius for handling people, but rather an acquired skill cultivated over his career. His home library overflows with books on management, more than a hundred dog-eared volumes.

As a statement of his management philosophy, Roger kept a sign in his office that simply said, "Think." He empowered employees to make good decisions, instead of attempting to limit their capacity to make bad ones. As Martino noted:

> *What Roger had was a skill to recognize other good investors...knowing when to recognize talent.*

Some people were really good at sales and bringing clients in; some people were good at innovation and thinking of different things that they could form to make investment products. He would let investment talent go in a way that allowed them to form portfolios.

Roger also often served as a guide, and a check, for the younger, more reckless partners, like Peter Foreman: "I would have a creative idea in my head, and I would go talk to Roger about it, and Roger would tell me, 'Don't waste your time.' Or 'That sounds interesting.' Roger was my sounding board, and he taught me an awful lot." Peter described him as psychologically acute: "He knows how to handle people. He knows how to read people. What they're good at, and what they aren't good at." He used this capacity skillfully to orchestrate the outcomes of decisions and meetings:

Roger never had a meeting that he didn't know what the outcome was that he wanted. And so, he would come to me on many occasions, and say, "Look, this is what I think." And he would kind of prep me so that I could be a foil as to helping him get to the outcome that he wanted in the meeting. He knew exactly where he was going, and he was able to guide us to the conclusion that he wanted.

However, as Gary Holzman observed, Roger's approach never felt coercive, even if he usually did get his way: "It's really one of the incredible qualities of Roger: the ability to get a team or group of people to follow his plan, and not have them feel like, 'Oh, I'm just a puppet and Roger's the puppeteer.' Instead, he really does that team building."

Peter Foreman recalls Harris as a cordial, supportive environment in the early days. In some respects, Roger's management was permissive, more so than one could get away with today. For example, in the mid-1980s, there was a rash of intra-office marriages. Upon the third such marriage, between Bill and Cynthia Nygren, Roger wrote to his family, "It's an exciting event in which Harris Associates has played a very important role of providing propinquity. We have also helped by hiring very bright, attractive people who are naturally mutually attracted to each other. This is the third internal marriage out of an organization of less than 60 people. So far we have handled the potential management problems by ignoring them." Harvard Business School likely won't teach this strategy in a casebook, but it worked for Harris Associates.

Roger's *laissez-faire* style sometimes surprised his employees. In the early years of Holzman's tenure, he brought in a draft memo for correction. Roger made a change or two and handed it back to him. Gary said, "Roger, I'm kind of surprised. I mean, I'm pleased that you're not making many changes. But I'm surprised." Roger replied, "Gary I could spend time tweaking things; I could put it in my voice. But what's the point? You're still getting the message across." As Holzman admitted, this management style yielded better results: "knowing that things aren't going to be micromanaged, you step up."

VALUE INVESTING AND TIGER HUNTS

Harris Associates is a value investor: it discovers underpriced businesses and invests in them. They find such bargains by studying the financial underpinnings as well as intangible qualities of a business, investing only after investigating its culture and management strategies, ensuring they worked with managers whose values closely aligned with their own. This approach, and the research underlying it, has allowed Harris Associates to make long-term investments instead of trying to profit on daily trading.

The firm began with a modest sum under management. As Peter Foreman recalled, "We asked Irv Harris; he had about 25 million dollars' worth of what I always called his cocktail party friends." The partners also invested their own money, not always profitably. Foreman found that some of their initial funds, like the Acorn Fund, continued to lose money even after Harris sold the business. It was Myron Szold, not Roger or Peter, who finally catalyzed the firm's rise:

> *Myron was managing some funds for one of the chief executives at Standard Oil in Indiana then. And he started shooting the lights out. And so, this guy started referring him to other people. And the business started growing very fast. We started getting institutional accounts.*

"And that's the Harris Associates story," Roger concluded. Perhaps this abbreviated narrative is justified; the firm's early rise seemed to him a continuous stream of luck. In 1986, when Harris Associates moved offices, Roger reflected on its past, present, and future: "We hope we will have as much good luck in our new offices as we have had in our present quarters where we have been for nine years. During this period of time our assets under management have multiplied by more than ten times. Our profits have also grown."

However, the business became increasingly complex and demanding as it grew. In the same letter, Roger recognized, "Our business now seems to be more difficult to manage because of changing goals and lifestyles of the key people of the business." In the mid-1980s, Roger oversaw a restructuring of the firm, transforming it from a corporation into a partnership, and inviting ownership from the next generation. He explained,

> Part of the restructuring was motivated for tax reasons...and the other cause was to recognize the values of the business and create permanent benefits for the former stock-holders. In doing this we also enhanced the capital ownership of the company in the hands of younger employees who eventually will own and control the business after partners retire.

If this restructuring empowered younger employees, it also gave them freedom to make decisions that Roger opposed, such as the sale of the firm in 1995 to the French firm Natixis. At the time, he described the sale as an "unfortunate mistake," though he understood:

> [H]aving money in the pocket is a tremendous
> incentive to the young partners who we brought into
> the partnership. Of course they are now experienced
> investors and believe that this is only the beginning
> of the fortune they will build by brilliantly investing
> their assets. We will see.

In 2020, Harris Associates had two hundred employees and 86 billion dollars under management. The firm has an international reputation; its funds have been ranked among the top mutual funds in the country.

Reflecting on this success, Roger has identified values that guided the company, including an entrepreneurial ethos and a tolerance for uncomfortable risks. In 1982, for example, Peter Foreman came to Roger with a plan to help institutional funds short stocks. It was a complicated transaction; First National Bank of Chicago had to give the firm an unsecured loan of $50 million. "I'm not very sure how comfortable Roger was with that," Peter admitted, "but we ran it for 10 years and it was very profitable. We made a bunch of money. I got queried a lot about 'wasn't this going to collapse on us?'"

As Peter recounted, "The business is a levered bet. If the market's up 10%, our fees go up 10% and our cost goes up 2%, so we don't need to own more stocks." As a way to diversify their assets and limit risk, "it worked very well," Peter said: "in the six years before I left, we were averaging 17% annualized growth with a third of the volatility of the S&P." Peter has forgiven Roger's initial skepticism concerning this and other daring ideas.

Roger told Peter once that their relationship was like a tiger hunt; in Peter's version,

> *I tell him, "Roger, you wait here, pitch the tent and wait." I'm gone 12 hours and Roger's getting nervous. I'm gone 24 hours, he's really upset. 36 hours he's tearing what hair he has on his head off. Then he sees me and I'm running as fast as I can run. And as I run by Roger, I tell him, "There's a live tiger right behind me and there's four more coming," and I go right out the other end of the tent. And that was the nature of our relationship. I created the problems or the ideas, and Roger figured out how to skin them and make them work.*

Peter, Roger, and Victor also established one of the early fund of funds, Aurora, in 1987. Roxanne Martino joined in 1990 and served as its CEO for 28 years. She had been working at Grosvenor Capital Management when she first met Roger; as she described it:

> *He and another partner of the firm came over to say, "After the crash of '87, we want to diversify our own capital away from the U.S. stock market. Can you help us invest in hedge funds in a diversified way?" At that time I had one partner at Grosvenor and we talked about it and we said, "They're going to do it with us or without us. And this is a great, talented group of people: let's do this together."*

Roxanne started at Harris in an office next door to Roger. The two collaborated closely in the early years of Aurora, building the fund's capital. She was impressed by Roger's disciplined approach to finding capital:

> *Every day, Roger would make a list of 10 people that he was going to call about this new entity. And he would say to me, "You just make a list. These are the people you're going to call. Call them in order. And you want to be done by noon. Don't go to lunch until you're done. It was simple: people put off things they don't want to do, or they're nervous about. He just was never that person: he just had discipline.*

Martino has emulated Roger: "I try to do things that might be more difficult in my day before noon. It doesn't matter what stage you're at. It's always useful to do that." For her, the early years at the firm were "thrilling...We had a 'creeping' vine approach to expanding our investor base: one happy investor telling another."

A HARD HEAD, A SOFT HEART

In January 1991, the partners at Harris gathered at the Wrigley Mansion on Lakeview Avenue to honor Roger's contributions to the firm. In a letter to the family, Roger described the event as "exquisitely catered. For example, the dessert was an apple torte in a crust basket with two crossing crust arches topped by a small ball of cinnamon ice cream. It resembled a regal crown and tasted good too." The dinner was followed by speeches from Myron,

Andrew, and Howard. Andrew was not expecting to speak: "I wish they had given me so much as an hour to prepare; they kind of just called on me, which was a bit anxiety-provoking, but I guess I pulled it off." Roger was particularly touched by Howard's remarks, writing to the family: "Uncle Howard's was by far the most outstanding during which he surpassed all his previous orations." In the speech, Howard represented his brother's character:

> *Roger, like all of us, became a crucible of contradictions...one might say, a hard head with a soft heart. The hard head addresses the pursuit of perfection, the thrust to excellence, the drive to succeed. The eyes in this hard head survey statistics, analyze accounting, measure earnings, apply hardcore engineering techniques. Yet this hard head is capped in moral and ethical considerations. "What's right, what's fair, what's reasonable? Is it the proper thing to do?"*

> *The soft heart describes a man who is generous, compassionate, kindly...a man sensitive to the human condition who realizes that ultimately chance not choice determines our destiny and that, beyond the diminishing returns generated by the pursuits of pleasures and possessions, one must replant his soul by giving to the community...*

The speech culminated in a gift from Howard and Betsy: eight framed photos of Roger in his early childhood and youth, which hung in Roger and Barbara's house for years afterward. At the close of the evening, all fourteen partners stood up and pledged a $250,000 donation to Thresholds for an endowment in Roger's name. Savoring the event in his weekly letter, he wrote, "I am beginning to think my life has been worthwhile." Still, ever on guard, he quickly added, "But I had better watch out of flattery and keep my feet on the ground. I still expect to be around for a long while and there is lots to do."

LUXURY AND THRIFT

When Roger left A.G. Becker in 1973, he was well on his way to achieving his childhood goal of wealth. 18 years later, when he retired from Harris Associates, he had more than achieved it. He was not only personally wealthy; he had made enough money to ensure his family's financial security, potentially for generations. Yet Roger's attitude toward his own wealth was ambivalent. On the one hand, he wrote in his "Confessions," "Now that I have achieved my goal of becoming rich, I admit that I have a feeling of accomplishment." On the other, he lamented the inequality of American society: "I never expected to be in the '1%' that has a disproportionately large percentage of income and assets in the United States. These differences in wealth are politically unsustainable." Owen explained his father's attitude:

> *I think that Roger was certainly interested in seeing the numbers accumulate in his various accounts, but actually for him, it became an intellectual exercise. He wanted to have enough money to do what he wanted*

TEMPLE OF LUXOR
February 1977
Roger & Barbara on vacation in Egypt

> *to do... But what he wanted to do was far more than
> the money he wanted to make. He wanted to create
> a dynasty, and he may have to a modest extent. Vast
> displays of wealth—Larry Ellison buying an island,
> supporting an America's Cup team—were flash. Just
> wasn't in his and Barbara's DNA.*

This is not to say that Roger was allergic to the trappings of wealth or luxury. When he was still working, he had expensive watches and suits, which he would wear in rotation until they wore out; in retirement, he paid for the entire family to vacation together at a Club Med in Cancún each year. Andrew noted, "Roger's never been shy about spending money...it's not like my parents bought a Hyundai, even if it works as well as a Lexus."

This willingness to spend on luxuries was balanced by a strain of thriftiness that runs through the family's history. In *Reminiscences*, Isidore related a story of Gladys' economizing. He needed cash to complete a real estate transaction in the early 1930s. He planned to borrow $10,000 from a bank and asked Gladys to co-sign. Gladys told him not to bother. She had $10,000 in hand from money she'd saved over the years by carefully budgeting her expenditures. Roger too had a thrifty streak. As Peter Foreman found, "He has no problem taking 45 people to Cancún for a week and paying for the whole damn thing. But he has a lot of trouble buying a five-cent candy bar that he thinks should sell for three cents." He has passed this habit down to younger generations of Browns.

In Joey's estimation,

> *He could very easily afford to replace his pants if he got a hole in them, but he doesn't. Barbara would put a patch on it. Which is something I guess I still do too. I probably could buy some new jeans every now and then. My parents get angry at me because I still wear a couple shirts from the Territory which they bought me at Water Tower Place in 2007. There were holes in them that I continue to get patched by my dry cleaners. Or the fact that right now I'm running a 2005 red Toyota Rav 4 straight into the ground; Roger is still doing that too with his cars.*

Andrew speculated that Roger's thrifty tendencies increased with age. In his retirement, he swapped his expensive watches for a cheap Timex and threadbare jeans that had to be tossed:

> *Much of his "thriftiness" emerged more so as he aged, as he wanted to set some example for his notoriously profligate children! Some of this was just crazy. Mom had to inevitably burn some ragged blue jeans. I told him on one occasion about 7 to 10 years back, while going to some social event, that he needed to change because he looked like a hobo. This pissed him off.*

THE FAMILY OFFICE

In June 1996, Roger attended a conference on family offices at the Intercontinental Hotel in Chicago. Writing to the family afterwards, Roger outlined the challenges that wealthy families face in securing their legacies:

> *One speaker, James Hughes, put our goal quite simply—each generation has to face the challenge of "shirtsleeves to shirtsleeves in three generations." Each is faced with the weights of 1. Malthusian expansion (multiple beneficiaries as families grow); 2. Inflation; 3. Taxation; 4. Divorces; and 5. Bad luck and/or poor management. The main job of the family office is to organize the family to preserve real wealth which means both earning assets and more important the ethical standards to inspire the younger generations to sustain the "people wealth" which is the strongest and most important asset needed for maintaining the family.*

In his letters, Roger was consistent on this point: the family's character and culture is more important than its material standing. In 1983, for example, he wrote, "Our confidence should not be based on our material position but on our skills in living and working with other humans, as well as the knowledge and know-how we have developed." The establishment of the Brown family office in 1997 served to reinforce the family's wealth as well as its values. In Roger's view, "The impetus behind these efforts was the belief that 'family' is important and that the results of working together could strengthen relationships and benefit all. I think this has proven to be the case."

Today, the office is engaged not only with Roger's children and grandchildren, but also with Howard's; it serves the financial interests of some fifty people, spread across the United States and beyond, and in all stages of life. It began on a lower floor at Harris Associates, then moved to an office shared with Peter Foreman at 225 West Washington, in downtown Chicago. Over its twenty-five-year existence, the office has depended on a steady, dedicated staff, beginning with Julie Vitiritti, who started working for Roger in 1993, before the family office was officially organized. Handling the accounting for the office and filing its taxes, Julie has become indispensable to the family's complicated financial life.

When the office was founded in 1997, Roger hired Gary Holzman as its executive director, luring him away from Arthur Andersen, where he had worked for eleven years. Gary and Roger collaborated to build a framework for the family office. As both the family and assets under management expanded, so did the office's head count, to include Barb Blacharczyk and Debbie Rahn as support staff, Jennifer Dobosh as controller, and most recently, Matthew Tupy as assistant controller. As Holzman recalled, "We started the office from scratch...Roger loves to build things, he loves to build businesses, loves to build teams of people. So this was his sweet spot. And as I told the family all the time: I get the best of Roger, and this is where he really thrives." Holzman, who continues to run the family office as of this writing, regards Roger as a mentor: "He cared a great deal about me as a person,

GARY HOLZMAN

Executive director of the Brown family office
since its founding in 1997

as an employee; he helped me be better at helping him and his family. It was never done in a hard-handed way. It has always been done in a constructive building-up and in a positive manner."

The family office was founded at a moment of exceptional prosperity. As Roger wrote in the mid-1990s, "The world of 1995 is full of opportunity. The political and economic background haven't been this good since before the beginning of World War I, ninety years ago." The Brown family office has weathered the ensuing storms, such as the 2008 financial crisis. Holzman remembered this as a difficult moment made better by Roger's clear-headed approach:

> *The portfolio was losing millions upon millions of dollars...And Roger was at his best. He was calm. He was supportive. And he was strategic. And other family offices, other people I know were running around just very unsettled. And in the most stressful time, he just became the rock, both for me and for the family.*

In the fall of 2008, Roger wrote to the family, at Owen's suggestion, to urge them to take this long perspective: "This is a trying period for investors. Don't panic and sell. You may be right for a few weeks, but you'll be wrong for the long term. These problems have happened before, and they always end." Roger consistently responded to crises with equanimity. After Black Monday in 1987, he offered the family similar advice: "Chances are things will work out all right, but a lot of people on the edge are going to suffer. In spite of all the uncertainty there should be good opportunities to make money—so be aware, be entrepreneurial and persist." He might have added "and resist," for when Roger was approached by Bernie Madoff, he refused a chance to invest in his fund. As Owen observed of the incident, "I think that in many ways he's a very good judge of others' characters; he showed a deeper understanding of possible consequences, either negative or positive... I don't know how he was able to develop this sense, but at least for some time he had it." For Joey, Roger's calm in the face of crisis reflected his historical perspective, his study of global patterns and trends: "While I don't think Roger would ever...fall back upon easy aphorisms like 'history repeats itself,' he does think about patterns in really broad and grand ways, and...that I think is not necessarily typical of others who have had professions like his."

Roger's composure has not always served him well. On September 11, Roger learned of the terrorist attacks on the Twin Towers as he was riding the elevator up to work; he remained in the office until mid-afternoon:

> *I had no concern that I was personally threatened, though we were receiving information that the Sears Tower was being evacuated and that trading on the Board of Trade, Options Exchange, and Merc were halted as was trading in New York... Regardless, I had work to do and though our office was emptying of people, I saw no reason to leave.*

Roger conceded that his behavior warranted concern from his family: "During the day, I received several phone calls from Andy suggesting that I was taking undue risks." Andrew recalled with exasperation:

> *This was a strange episode...He was not really monitoring the situation well. He did not realize or accept that there was a high probability that hijackers were going to fly a plane into the Sears Tower, which is close to his office. He was being, frankly, obstinate and stubborn, which seriously distressed my wife at the time, for which I think he felt guilty afterwards, because it was unnecessary and he didn't have work that was critical. What could be critical? Wall Street's closed, man; the World Trade Center just collapsed.*

The family office kept Roger busy in retirement; four days a week, he took the Metra downtown from Highland Park to work with Gary, preparing for the next generation to take charge of the family's fortunes. Gary described this chapter of Roger's legacy:

> *In his eighties he realized he's not going to live forever, so we dispersed the authority across the family. We have the investment committee, the family office management committee. Roger had one vote, but his vote was a big vote. Little by little other people felt empowered, so we built a family office that will outlast him. That's really another kind of success for him...that he managed to build a second layer that will keep going.*

THOSE LESS FORTUNATE

In 2018, beholding his fortunes, Roger wrote to the family: "Let's look at it realistically; I am 92, Mom is 89, we've accumulated more money than we'll ever need. Maybe we can find some good use of it, other than taking the profit incentive out of the lives of our children and grandchildren." Since his youth, Roger had dreamed of being rich enough to be independent, and to be in a position to help others. The family's charity has been wide-ranging and diverse, supporting prestigious causes as well as under-the-radar social service agencies on the West Side of Chicago.

Long before the family office was established, the Browns founded the I & G Charitable Foundation, named for Isidore and Gladys. Roger "had hoped that the I & G would be a great family unifying learning space for philanthropy. And my kids have worked just lately on governance issues there, which excites me that they may be willing and able to continue the I & G." The foundation serves as one of the remainder beneficiaries for Barbara's and Roger's estates. I & G—along with the 1261 Foundation, a family Donor Advised Fund housed at Chicago's Jewish Community Foundation—now has $13 million under management. Together, the two annually donate approximately $900,000 to charity.

Before and alongside I & G, Roger has given generously to a range of causes and institutions, including the scientific and ecological initiatives that Barbara cherished. The couple gave money and time to the Chicago Botanic Gardens and the Field Museum. In addition to her work as a researcher, Barbara served on the women's board at the Field Museum for more than four decades, beginning in 1974; her niece, Amy Brown Tuchler, and two of her daughters-in-law, Gail Feiger Brown and Cindy Scalzo, later joined her. For Barbara's birthday in 2009, Roger made a major donation to the Botanic Gardens to create a 12-acre nature preserve on their grounds.

The area, a small pond just north of Dundee road, was one of Barbara's favorites, a place where she spent many days watching shorebirds and rails. Invasive buckthorn and garlic mustard had overrun the grounds. Roger's gift allowed the Botanic Gardens to build trails, root out invasive species, and create new habitat for birds, drag-onflies, butterflies, frogs, and insects. Dedicated in 2011, the area ensures that Barbara's name will live on at the Botanic Gardens.

In 2018, the couple also made a two-million-dollar donation to the Science Museum of Minnesota (the larg-est donation in the museum's history), which endowed a new research position, the Barbara Brown Chair of Ornithology. They had visited the museum several times: Alison Brown, Owen's wife, is its CEO. Barbara saw an opportunity to strengthen its research wing. The museum recently hired Catherine Early as its first Barbara Brown Chair. The chair not only oversees the museum's biology department and conducts research and fieldwork; she also works to attract the general public to the museum.

Roger has, of course, been a generous and long-term donor to Exeter. In 1973, the family established the Howard J. Brown '42 Scholarship Fund to augment the school's capacity to offer financial aid. In 1979, in honor of Isidore's 90th birthday, they created a fund in Isidore and Gladys' name to buy books for the school's library. In 1985, they established an award to honor the best teachers at the school, the Brown Family Faculty Fund. In structuring these gifts, Roger gave careful thought to how his gifts might do the most good. In 1985, he described the goals of the Faculty Fund:

> *The purpose is basically to pay more money to the better teachers. This is hard to do in educational institutions and the device of a discretionary fund is to help this goal. Theoretically the money may have some influence in attracting, retaining, and motivating a faculty that over time may easily lose its energy and enthusiasm.*

These contributions show Roger's commitment to transforming Exeter's culture. During the 1950s, he wrote a series of letters to the school and its alumni council, urging them to integrate the school more quickly and more deeply. Owen summarized his father's motivations:

> *Nobody told him to do this. He just felt it was the right thing to do. Not that he didn't suffer the prejudices of the age, but he believed in a meritocracy that was built on capabilities and was able to look beyond racial prejudices that he may have been born with. For example, I had a black boss when I was interning at a division of Sears, who had been a colonel in the Army, and I think Roger liked him a fair amount because of his Army record. So he said, "Oh, this guy knows how to do stuff, and who cares*

if he's black." That was Roger. If you could do it,
didn't matter your color, your religion, probably
your sex. You had to be able to do it. That was it.

Through Owen's eyes, Roger was "economically conservative, but socially liberal," a politics manifested in his
eclectic philanthropy. Roger has regularly given to well-
known institutions like the University of Chicago and
Jewish United Fund; in 1994, he reported that these were
the largest recipients of his philanthropy for the previous
year. But Roger has also given time and money to what
Owen calls "dirty causes" such as "prisoners' rights, vets
with mental problems, early childhood intervention in
extremely poor neighborhoods. He doesn't want to give
to country club charities, because the opera is not suffering. He wanted to, still wants to, alleviate suffering."

Roger has long championed Thresholds, a Chicago-
based social service agency for people suffering from
mental illness—including, in recent years, veterans returning from Iraq and Afghanistan with PTSD. When Roger
got involved, Thresholds was led by the forward-thinking
mental health expert, Jerry Dincin. Dincin had started his
career as a furniture salesman in New York City, working
in his family business. In 1958, he took a job working
at Fountain House, a rehabilitation center for mentally
ill people. At the time, psychiatric care wasn't widely
available; people with mental illness were released from
hospitals and clinics with nowhere to go. Fountain House
offered them a place to stay; it helped them find jobs and
housing. In 1965, Jerry came to Chicago to become the
executive director of Thresholds. Then housed in a dumpy

office on Dearborn street, the organization only had a few employees. Roger remembered, "You could smell the rats running around through the place. You couldn't see any of them, but you figured that it would make a nice home." Jerry convinced the board to follow the Fountain House model. Under Jerry's leadership, Thresholds expanded to become, in Roger's estimation, "gigantic." By the time Dincin retired in 2002, the organization had more than 900 employees and served more than 6,000 people struggling with mental illness, addiction, and homelessness.

Early in Dincin's tenure, Mary Hill—a Thresholds board member and the wife of one of Roger's Harvard classmates, Mike Hill—obtained a list of potential donors from her husband and sent Roger a letter asking for a donation. After Roger made a modest contribution, she asked him to join the board. By 1972, Roger was spearheading a $500,000 capital campaign to buy an old school building and convert it. He eventually served as president of the board; he convinced friends and business partners like John Mabie and Roxanne Martino to get involved, sometimes through subterfuge. Early in her tenure at Harris Associates, Roger invited Roxanne to lunch, so she thought:

> So we're walking. I said, "Oh, where are we going to lunch?" He brought me to a Thresholds meeting. It was a box lunch. And he said, "I think you would want to know about Thresholds." Well, that changed the course of my life without a doubt because I sat in that back row with him eating this box lunch.

BARBARA & ROGER WORKING AT THE HOUSE

Late 1950s

A rare event for Roger, who would rather pay someone else to garden

"It's very Roger," Martino laughed, "Roger is very frugal." Yet, Roger's ruse paid off; Roxanne became a passionate supporter of Thresholds: "I thought, 'This is what I should be doing with my time and my talents, so I got involved in Thresholds. I joined the board shortly thereafter and here I am, 30 years later, I'm still on the board and still on the executive committee."

When Roger retired from the presidency of Thresholds' board, Isidore and Gladys established a fund there in his name. Even after Roger stopped soliciting, Thresholds remained an important part of his life. Owen recounted, "We were able to leverage his 90th birthday to raise two hundred and fifty thousand dollars from family and friends for the institution. It was a big surprise for him!"

Alongside Thresholds, Roger got involved in the early 2000s with another so-called "dirty cause," St. Leonard's Ministries, which helps people reestablish their lives once they leave prison. Bob Dougherty, the organization's Executive Director, recalled that Roger approached him:

> *I didn't solicit him. I didn't even know who he was, but a third-party friend in the for-profit world knew Roger. She suggested, well, "you should come to St. Leonard's." So we met. And at first, I thought, "My gosh, he's a crusty little guy." He's rather direct; however, I believe that turned out to be what he liked about St. Leonard's. I could be just as direct as he could be.*

St. Leonard's focuses on reducing recidivism rates, which are nearly 43% in Illinois, but under 13% among those served by St. Leonard's. For Roger, Dougherty explained,

> *The statistics spoke for themselves. And I think he liked the way we did it because we did it not just to reduce numbers, but to rebuild people. And when you rebuild people, then you've given them an opportunity to move to the positive side of the ledger. We had several philosophical talks about St. Leonard's and the people who come there: if there's any hope for them. And that's certainly what we believed. And I realized that's what Roger believed.*

Roger's belief in rehabilitation exhibits his outlook on life: a guarded optimism, a careful faith in the capacity of human beings to fix their own and each other's problems. In February 2020, when asked during an interview whether he thought the 45th president would allow a peaceful transition of power, since "some say he'll have to be dragged out of the White House," Roger responded simply with a defiant laugh, "Well, let's do it."

He believed that the world is largely moving in the right direction and that people are mostly good: "I just think the human nature of leadership will solve these problems." Owen explained his father's worldview:

> *Generally, he's a pessimist, or a realist. But I think in his long life and his understanding of history, he's seen that the worst generally does not come to*

pass. Now maybe it will with climate change, but he went through the Lloyd's of London meltdown, and it was not nearly as bad as people thought it was going to be, and so on, so forth. And so, he thinks, and I think quite rightly so, that there's an attempt to dramatize and look for the worst and generally that doesn't happen. And that's why he is somewhat optimistic: things will change and somehow you'll survive.

BROWN & BROWN

Novemeber 25 2010

Roger shortly after the family office was established

Chapter 5

GOLDEN AGE

WHILE ROGER BUILT HARRIS ASSOCIATES, then the family office, his family was in transition: the elders beginning to pass on; the children beginning to rise into maturity. Roger's letters record these changes, celebrating moments of joy and accomplishment; meditating and commiserating through grief and crisis. For all their varied concerns—from tennis to French, opera to economics— Roger's letters are, at heart, a record of his family's life. But they are not intimate or tender documents: Roger's tendency was to report, advise, and admonish.

The letters bear witness to complications in Roger's relationships—his habit of teasing, his relative absence from his children's early lives—even as he expresses joy at observing their growth and accomplishments. In January 1975, for instance, he wrote to his sons:

> *This Christmas holiday was unique because everyone was home for the full period. For me it was a joyous occasion. It rather reminds me of the forecast I got from a fortune cookie at the Dragon Inn North—"Your life will be one of prosperity and contentment." Each of you contributed to the success of this vacation both by the things you did as well as those you didn't do. Though to you, the evolution of your personalities and attributes may appear as viscous as molasses, it is much more apparent to your elders whose psychological chronologies are much faster than those of younger generations.*

We can see you maturing in behavior, attitude, appearance, and relationships; and we note this in the most difficult and trying relationships—with your parents and siblings.

Eight years later, Vanessa's confirmation at Temple Jeremiah in 1983 evoked a similar outpouring of paternal pride, despite fractures that marred the relationship between father and daughter:

Vanessa was dressed in a lovely red and gray striped dress and gray shoes. She looked stunning and gave a distinguished confirmant's speech disclosing what it means to her to be a Jew and why she chose to be confirmed as one...I was beaming with happiness throughout the ceremony. It is great to have raised a family that wants to be together and stay together. May it ever remain so and may they, in turn, have families that feel the same way toward each other.

The confirmation was followed by a dinner cooked at home by Barbara and Vanessa. Roger ruminated:

Though the ceremony was touching and the event that it celebrated personally satisfying—looking backward it is also an indication of the tremendous, good fortune we have had that our grandfathers or great grandfathers had the gumption and courage to start life anew in this great country. We Jews are now in a golden age in the United States that probably cannot be compared to anytime or place in our 5,000-year history.

This meditation on Jewish history is touching, if removed from the immediate experience of Roger's children. While in this letter Vanessa's celebration yields to historical abstraction, elsewhere Roger could be attentive to the specificities of his children's lives, the mundane disappointments and struggles they encountered as they entered the workforce. In the spring of 1983, he wrote:

What an unusual set of circumstances. Three of our sons are looking for jobs—and what a terrible time to be released to a stuttering economy where businesses don't want to pay for business school graduates and many are still in a contraction phase, cutting back on employment so that their costs can be competitive. It's never pleasant looking for jobs and now is even a more trying time...Keep trying, persist, you will succeed. Don't expect anything to drop in your lap even though it might.

Roger's children respected his opinions and valued his counsel. At a professional crossroads in 1997, Owen wrote asking for career advice, which Roger warmly gave:

It's wonderful that you are seeking the advice of your family concerning your next career move...I think your occupational choices reflect deeply on your own personal goals and desires to which we are not privileged. Dealing in this area may be a sensitive activity in which you may not want your loved ones to "honestly" give their opinions. Regardless, I think it is courageous for you to ask. Though you may have had several unsuccessful business experiences, do not underestimate the value of those activities…You have done lots of different things and experienced how a variety of businesses and people operate and think. This knowledge and experience is irreplaceable and extremely valuable. It would be a wasted asset not to use in some fashion.

Remembering the "difficulties" of his father's love from the safe distance of adulthood, Owen saw Roger as typical; his parenting, a reflection of the standards of the day, rather than a character flaw, though Owen too remained perturbed by Roger's teasing.

Roger worked very hard and was largely absent during the majority of my childhood, as many fathers of that era were. Then I was sent off to Exeter when I was 14, and so by and large my contact with him was on the more modest side. We would go to his den when he wanted to talk to us, which was on occasion. Roger had his good sides and his bad sides. He'd tease us mercilessly, which was something that you shouldn't do to any child, but when he praised us it was something that you really felt great about. At least, I did. We knew that he loved us, or I knew that he loved me, even though sometimes I felt that there were difficulties in that love, and it was combined with disappointment.

AT HOME

Late 1990s

Roger & Barbara

As his children grew up, started their own careers, and had their own children—beginning with Tamara in 1980—Roger had time to think about parenting, the realities of which he had mostly escaped during the 1950s and 1960s. After babysitting two of his granddaughters for an evening in 1986, he wrote:

> *I am now beginning to understand why so many women are now returning to the work force after giving birth to their children...Taking care of two or three youngsters requires constant attention, patience and a high degree of tolerance, much less of which is needed in the daily pressures at work. Commuting is no fun, but dealing with the boss and worrying about work problems is a wonderful diversion from dirty diapers, messy feeding, toys strewn around the house...*

These encounters with the messy work of parenthood do not seem to have induced a reevaluation of Roger's own fathering, even when he was directly challenged on the matter. In a letter from 1985, Roger reported a dinner-table dispute with Betsy:

> *Dinner was excellent; however, during it Betsy and I got into a heated argument about how I should treat my children. Naturally she has an opinion about what was best for them and predicted maleficent results from my parenthood. Fortunately she didn't understand all the facts including the main one— which is that often I make noise but that Barbara*

has raised our children. Looking backward—and also ahead—I feel very confident in the outcome of what we have done and frankly I think Betsy does too.

THE MEANING OF LIFE

Despite his complex relationships with his own children, Roger greeted the arrival of his grandchildren with jubilation, a joy shared across generations. In *Reminiscences*, Isidore described seeing Tamara for the first time: "For me, life's whole joyous meaning is to be found in that girl's precious little smile." Upon Ariana's birth in 1983, Roger wrote to the family:

> *Welcome Ariana. Everyone is eager to see you, to hold you, to hear you coo, to watch you eat and sleep and grow and learn. To teach you to crawl and walk and talk and play. Ariana joined life on earth at 3:15 a.m. Friday, March 25, at Michael Reese Hospital. She weighed 7 lbs. 13 oz, and is a healthy normal baby.*

Over the succeeding months, Roger's letters frequently returned to Ariana. On Mother's Day that year, after describing Barbara's "chicken in ginger cream sauce" and Tamara's shy reaction to the clutch of adults ("she coyly held on to Daddy Jeffrey's leg for thirty minutes to help her build her self-confidence") Roger concluded, "But of greatest note was the outstanding behavior of Ariana, who traveled from one set of arms to another, posing for pictures, watching lips curled for cooing sounds, and calmly enjoying her moments of grandeur."

In July, joy turned to anxiety, as Ariana was admitted into the NICU with viral meningitis: "She was close to death early last week with inadequate breathing and heartbeat. Luckily, Jennifer identified the severity of her illness." Before the week was out, Ariana had returned home. The crisis had an unexpected benefit for Roger and Barbara, granting them a week babysitting Tamara. As Roger reported to the family,

> *The other chapter of the story is Miss Tamara Martine Brown. She is a pumpkin. Highly articulate, sympathetic personality, reasonable requests, good sense of humor, quick to learn and loads of fun. We all love her more and more every time we are with her and feel lucky that we were privileged to have her until Monday evening when Jeff will come to pick her up. We can guess how much she must have been missed. But it won't be long till Ariana is just as cute and before you know it, they'll both be in their terrible teens. Enjoy the compliant playfulness while you can—after a while they won't pay any attention to you or may become adversaries in spirit.*

Soon Tamara and Ariana were so closely joined that Roger began referring to them as a single unit, *Tamariana*. In 1985, they were joined by Isaac, whose birth Roger dutifully recounted the next day:

Isaac Martin Brown is now one day old. Our first grandson, the bearer of a remarkable name, specifically honoring his great grandfather... The events surrounding the announcement were also rather dramatic. Uncle Howard, in his deep warmth of consideration, suggested that it would be nice if we all watched the sixth game of the "cross Missouri" World Series with Isidore on Saturday night. It was the last half of the 9th inning with St. Louis leading 1-0 in what appeared would become the last game of the series. Kansas City was filling up the bases when Jeffrey finally reached us to give us the news. Possibly we cheered more loudly with the news than the fans in Kansas City when they scored the winning run... Oh, what a great day!

In some respects, Roger's grandfathering reprised the dynamics of his relationship with his own children. As Aaron Brown described their bond,

I feel like, when I was a younger kid, I didn't really know how to connect with him super well. He always seemed a little, I don't know if "removed" is the right word, just his interests were always very adult. And the things that he liked and the things that we, as kids, liked didn't always match up. I think as I grew older, particularly when we became high school and college students, there were a lot more shared grounds to connect on. And then we were able to talk about things that he found interesting that I also found interesting.

MOTHER'S DAY

1968, 1261 Clavey Road

Min, Isidore, Gladys, Abe, Howard, Roger, & Barbara

Once his grandchildren entered adulthood, Roger carefully tracked their intellectual and professional developments. Eliza Brown, who holds a PhD in sociology, recalled Roger's enthusiasm for her work:

> *I think he's a very curious person and he likes to learn more about the state of the field and he certainly is knowledgeable about the last half century of sociology. He asks questions about specific and general social trends and always is sort of interested to hear about what my wife and I are studying.*

In addition to bonding over shared intellectual pursuits, Barbara and Roger established traditions, formal and informal, to bring and keep the family together. For example, they took each grandchild on a trip to commemorate their bar or bat mitzvah. Jacob Brown described one such trip:

> *One of my strongest memories with my grandpa was after my cousin and my B'nai Mitzvah. We, the four of us, went to Williamsburg, Virginia, and toured colonial America. A really strong memory that I have, Eliza and I still talk about, was when we were there, the thing that he wanted the most was to get a McDonald's milkshake and fries.*

Watching his grandchildren celebrate their bar and bat mitzvahs reminded Roger of the family's generational progress, and his own evolving role in it. In 2001, he wrote to the family:

> *While attending Aaron's bar mitzvah last weekend,*
> *I suddenly became confronted with the reality*
> *that my children are mature adults. It's not that I*
> *didn't realize this before, but with Tamara about to*
> *graduate from college and Aaron's development, the*
> *babies of the past are now the adults of today.*

Roger greeted this progression with equanimity; declaring his feelings in 2001, he wrote, "We are confident of their futures and proud of the fine job their parents have done." Roger began to serve as a bridge to the family's past. As Nicola recalled,

> *I went to the University of Chicago for undergrad.*
> *I have a nice memory of when Roger and Barbara*
> *drove down to Hyde Park to attend a lecture, and*
> *I went to lunch with them. Afterwards, we walked*
> *around the neighborhood for a little while, and*
> *Roger pointed out the apartment building where*
> *he'd lived as a child and talked a bit about his time*
> *there and the other kids who lived in the building.*

EBB AND FLOW

As Roger's children matured, his own parents' health began to decline. Gladys had been in failing health since the mid-1970s, with frequent trips to the hospital for conditions affecting her eyes, ears, thyroid, skin, and nerves. Throughout these spells of ill health, Isidore remained devoted to her, visiting her in the hospital each morning and again each afternoon. February 1986 found her in

Saint Joseph's Hospital in Lincoln Park, recovering from an infection. Roger summarized her condition:

> *Grandma Gladys has been sent to St. Joseph's Hospital because of a urinary infection. This seems to have passed, but she refuses to eat or communicate. Presently she is being fed intravenously, but we wonder if she is not sending us a message. Isidore has been visiting her regularly and is distraught, yet understanding of this condition and his inability to influence future events. There is little one can do but wait.*

Observing Gladys in this condition prompted Roger's universal meditations on mortality:

> *As time moves ahead and the beauty of the world continues to unfold, we watch the changing of seasons and the movement of events in man's perception of them. Terminal problems seem to concentrate one's mind on issues beyond the petty temporal goals and problems of the day. Yet the human mind is very facile and shifts back quickly to the present, subduing the deep and unanswerable problems into a compartment of memory where they cannot interfere with the need of survival and perpetuation. And just as human life ebbs and flows, so do the events of the day.*

Gladys recovered and returned home with Isidore. But, at the end of September that year, she finally passed.

She was 90 years old and had been married to Isidore for 66 years. In a letter to the family written after her death, Roger described theirs as "an ideal marriage." In November of 1986, shortly after her funeral, he realized,

> *Gladys' death brings to reality the fact that I am an adult who after these 60 years has to navigate as my own captain. Yes, I've managed to avoid the major shoals, but with it all I have had to live with myself and my imperfections, personality quirks and bad habits. One wonders whether the good overweighs the bad. I think so, and as a majority of one, I have unanimously concluded to continue on with the hope that I still have time to decrease the bad and increase the good.*

As Isidore wrote in *Reminiscences*, "the greatest gift that a father can give to the children is to love their mother." Reminded of this line in an interview with bioGraph, Roger laughed approvingly, "Ha! Well, I don't think we had a problem there."

In January of 1987, a few months after Gladys passed, Isidore closed his office to conduct his remaining work at home. In early May of 1988, he fainted and fractured his hip socket. Both of his legs had to be continually elevated to aid the healing of the damaged socket, causing circulatory problems. "Age is catching up with his body," Roger wrote, "but his spirits are high." One could find Isidore then in Room 746 at St. Joseph's Hospital, reading hungrily. As Roger observed, his other appetites remained active as well: "While he is in the hospital, he is having his ears and eyes examined to be sure everything is in good working order. Then…beware nurses."

In June, Isidore needed surgery to amputate his right leg just before the knee. Initially, the operation appeared to be a success. He went into surgery on a Friday; Roger saw him and visited with him that weekend. But on Wednesday, Roger received a call from Dr. Levy saying he had transferred Isidore to the intensive care unit. Barbara had returned from a trip to Israel earlier that day; she and Roger went to the hospital together for a final visit. On Thursday morning, the hospital called. Barbara answered the phone and learned that Isidore was gone. He was 98. The funeral was held on a Friday. Roger described the mournful scene in a letter:

> *Rabbi Howard Berman led the mourners and as his mellifluous and sonorous voice began the traditional lamentations I became emotionally overwhelmed. Barbara grasped me firmly and held on until my sobbing subsided. In the meantime Tamara, Ariana, and Isaac were quietly observing the ceremony, probably their first. Howard gave an eloquent eulogy followed by a poem read by Jules Dashow. We then recited the Mourner's Kaddish…then the cemetery workmen began lowering the casket bringing up a front end loader tractor to lower the lid of the cover. This intrigued Isaac. We all joined in dropping flowers or shoveling earth into the grave and said goodbye to Isidore.*

Following the service, the family gathered at Roger and Barbara's for dinner and games with three generations of Brown's: frisbee keepaway (a favorite of Howard's), shark, and running bases. Roger had taken Owen, Andy, and Henry on a trip to British Columbia earlier that year, during which salmon were caught, frozen, and brought back to Highland Park. The fish, alongside a double chocolate cake baked by Barbara and Vanessa, formed the basis for a large memorial meal. "It was a joy to be all together," Roger wrote, "to be healthy and to have the confidence that we loved one another."

With Isidore, an era passed. He had served as a master in chancery in Cook County Circuit Court for forty-two years—then a record. He was a lawyer for more than seventy years. In a letter from June 19, 1988, Roger accepted his father's death and planned for the future:

> *Isidore's death was not a tragic event. He was the patriarch of a "successful" family. He was a generous, thoughtful, yet demanding boss. He had his own way and his own ideas. You couldn't fool him or expect that he would condone an average performance. He was a professional flatterer and loved to classify people (especially his grandchildren) into life-type niches from which they may have had trouble escaping... To date I personally have not felt a deep grief at his loss. Some of my friends have noted that I will have periods of it. I think of him every day and when I see some of his handwritten letters I know I will never see his writing again. However, I feel that Howard and I lived up to my parents'*

expectations and continuously paid attention to our
parents in a way that leaves me with no feeling of
guilt or emptiness for actions I should have taken...
Our task now is to be as helpful as possible to
our children, grandchildren and eventually great-
grandchildren, so that they can face our death with
the same equanimity.

YOUR BRAIN STAYS ACTIVE

In 1991, on the eve of his 66th birthday, Roger wrote to his family, "I feel very happy about myself, my health, my family, my associates, and most everything about me." By this time Roger had been retired for almost a year. He and Barbara had spent that year engaged in the quotidian pleasures of family life, inaugurating a rhythm they sustained through the next thirty years: they drove up to Minnesota to see Vanessa's paintings in a show at Macalester College; they went to the opera; Roger returned to his morning tennis games, sometimes playing rather too hard, as he regretted in a letter from May 1991: "Yesterday was busy because I foolishly played from 8:30 to 11:30 in warm sunshine and spent much of the day suffering from cramps brought on by this excess." Until recently, Roger continued to hone his tennis game with lessons. His yearly bet with Howard, over which brother could best the other on the court, continued too. Several of Roger's children and grandchildren have also enjoyed tennis and have had the pleasure of attending tournaments together. As Aaron Brown recollected:

PROUD FATHER & BUSINESS MAN

Isidore one brisk day before
the apartment on Cornell Road

Among my favorite adult memories with [Roger and Barbara] is going out to BNP Paribas, the tennis tournament in Palm Springs, California. That was great because it was me and my cousin Joey as young adults going out with them to a thing that they really loved, and getting this opportunity to see really world-class tennis, stuff that I don't think either of us would've necessarily sought out. And getting to connect with them on the things we were doing as adults and talking with them on that level was always really nice.

Though retirement freed Barbara and Roger to connect on new levels with their grandchildren, business and philanthropy demanded their energies. Roger regretted not having more time for other pursuits: "There are books I would really like to read, but periodicals and business reading prevent anything but television and tennis. I feel guilty as my brain turns to mush. I am failing as an intellectual." For her part, Barbara continued working two days a week at the Field Museum and leading birdwatching walks at the Botanic Gardens: "If you keep active," she liked to say, "your brain stays active."

Practicing what Barbara preached, Roger and Barbara embarked on an ambitious program of travel. Travel had always been an important aspect of Brown family life; witness Isidore and Gladys' wide-ranging excursions. Barbara and Roger had taken their children on international trips from an early age, introducing them to a world beyond Highland Park. In 1968, they pulled Owen and Andy out of school and flew to Mexico City for the

Olympics. Andrew reminisced about the trip: "I had broken my wrist maybe about two weeks or so before we left. And I had a massive cast on my right arm. So it became a quest as we would go to different Olympic events to see if we could get different athletes to sign my cast. That was kind of funny and fun." Not that they were illicit "autograph hounds," Andrew clarified: they "had already pre-purchased these tickets to see a variety of events and activities."

Retirement allowed Roger and Barbara to travel more often and more adventurously. In the 1990s, they explored Belgium, France, Indonesia, Viet Nam, Italy, Hong Kong, Turkey, and France again, among other places. For each trip, Roger composed a richly-detailed travel diary. When Owen was spending a year abroad in Spain in the early 1970s, Roger instructed him how best to record his journey: "I can't emphasize how important you will find it in later life to take pictures of your experiences... Don't waste your time with scenery or works of art. Take pictures of people, including family, classmates, teachers, guides, girlfriends, musicians, etc. Also take pictures of your home, school, restaurants you frequent and places you may wish to remember." In Roger's experience, landmarks and tourist attractions should not distract from the purpose of travel: to gain cultural capital by sincerely connecting with places and people.

On his 2009 trip to Iran, for instance, Roger paid careful attention to the attitudes of young Iranians toward their government: "We had an Iranian female guide in the afternoon, Baran, who answered a number of questions about the social life of Tehran. The younger generation (the median age of the population is about 26) feel oppressed under the theocracy of the Ayatollah and they are not compliant with all the wishes of their more religious parents."

Roger's diaries are by turns philosophical, political, and grandfatherly; full of morality but never moralizing. His 1996 Italian travel diary begins with "two bits of good news."

> *Eliza called to let us know that Madeline is potty trained, well almost, once in a while she has an accident, but she sits on the potty and seems rather successful. But the second bit is really important. Eliza found her old blanket. It was in a bag on top of her dresser that she hadn't looked in "for many years." Although it's only a little rag now, she wants to keep it close to her all the time because she likes it so much. Could anything be nicer?*

On his trip to Iran, by contrast, Roger's attention turned to the country's history and its tense relationship with the United States:

> *In reviewing our trip both Mom and I had the distinct impression that we were audiences for a smooth marketing presentation by the representatives of the countries we visited. These are all totalitarian states with varying degrees of repressive governance. Though Iranians claim to like Americans—they still occupy the building that housed our Embassy and mouth destructive slogans about the U.S. Regardless,*

it is important to dialogue with all these important dictators whether we like them or not. I believe that Hillary Clinton and Obama have a heavy burden of diplomatic negotiations facing them, both in the Middle East and Asia.

This trip informed Roger's opinions on Iran, leading him in unexpected directions, despite his moderate conservative politics. As Joey recalled, however, Roger always strived for an independent worldview, regardless of party:

The public fervor and attitude towards Iran was probably much more negative than his. [As a result of his travels, Roger,] not even begrudgingly, was in support of the Barack Obama nuclear deal with Iran later on. I don't think that he was interested or prepared to take other people's opinions and present them as his own; he was sort of happy to go see these sorts of places for himself.

As Roger entered his ninth decade, he remained curious, open-minded, and intellectually engaged in politics.

In addition to Roger and Barbara's trips, they established a tradition of family travel: at winter break, as many members of the Brown family who could make it would gather at an all-inclusive resort for a few days of rest and relaxation. The family visited a number of these, eventually favoring one sponsored by Club Med in Cancun. As the years have gone by, these trips inspired their own small traditions, including various book clubs, games of Scrabble, and all fifty-odd family members eating dinner together at the end of the day. Roger's niece Sally recalled another tradition, which was launched on a smaller trip to Peru, with only fifteen or so Browns in attendance, but continued on the larger family trips:

> *We were having Pisco sours; I think I was in college. And fun Latin music is playing, and Roger and I started salsa dancing. Neither of us knew how to salsa dance. But he just was playful. He wanted to go for a spin on the dance floor and I wanted to do it too. And we just danced together. And so that became a common thing that we would do on vacation together. We would just lighten the mood and it would be a fun time.*

Roger delighted in these family trips, albeit in his guarded way, writing simply, "These [trips] have been very successful, especially our visits to Iberostar and Club Med."

AN INTERESTING STORY

The circle of Barbara and Roger's activities gradually tightened as their ages advanced. After 2010, their travel diaries decreased in number. This contraction of their lives was, in one sense, literal: as Roger wrote in a letter from February 2017, "My pants have become too long; or more honestly put, I have been shrinking. I think I have lost two inches since I was in the Navy 70 years ago...I hope that I don't shrink anymore."

In 2017, with Barbara's 88th birthday approaching, Roger wrote to the family:

> *It's hard to believe in three days Mom will be 88 years old. That's a long time, and when you combine that with my 91 years, there is a lot of long term genetic power that our kids may inherit. Maybe they may not want to live so long, but Barb and I are both enjoying our aging processes, especially as we have Gail and Amy nearby. You should be as lucky.*

Roger was clear-eyed and unsentimental about the costs of aging. After a 2018 spine surgery, which required several weeks of recuperation at home, he wrote, "I think that my main concentration will be on my health which is generally OK, but Mom has some serious problems that must be attended to. These are the results of growing old. We haven't bought our cemetery lots yet, but the old reaper will catch us sooner or later."

Despite the unflustered tone of the letter, Roger was wounded by a series of deaths in the family. In the beginning of April 2011, Howard was diagnosed with stomach cancer. Through the month, he continued to sustain the usual routines and activities—attending the family's Passover Seder and the board meeting for the United Communications Corporation (UCC), the media company Howard had founded. At its peak, UCC owned two daily newspapers, two weeklies, two shoppers, and two television stations, among them the *Kenosha Daily News*, which Howard published for four decades. These meetings had sometimes been sites of conflict between the

CANCUN

Early 2000s
Roger & Barbara, with Betsy & Howard
Roger was engrossed in McPherson's
study of Lincoln on that trip

brothers—with Howard's approach to business, motivated by his sense of loyalty to his employees, clashing with Roger's analytic approach. However, boardroom disagreements did not seriously disturb the deep affection the brothers had for each other.

Howard succumbed to his illness at the end of April. In addition to his long service as the owner of the *Kenosha Daily News*, he had graduated from Princeton University and the Columbia School of Journalism; he had been a stringer for the *Sun-Times* in Europe, the Near East, and Asia after World War II; he had worked for newspapers across the Midwest in advertising, circulation, and promotional capacities. Howard's was a life of engagement and accomplishment. In a small book prepared for a family reunion in 1990, Howard wrote, "Perhaps it is the mission of the journalist to discover and condense life's meaning. After 42 years one might suggest that it all comes together in these four sentences...Man lives. Man suffers. Man dies. But it is an interesting story. Telling that story is the journalist's calling."

Howard was loved by his family and respected by the Kenosha community. His death touched greater Kenosha. Eight hundred people attended his public memorial at Carthage College in May, including most members of the Brown family. The Carthage Wind Orchestra played Mahler's "Adagio" and Mozart's "Adagio K. 261"—two of his favorite pieces of music. Lucy Brown Minn, Steven Minn, Amy Brown Tuchler, Kenneth Dowdell, and Rabbi Dena Feingold offered reflections on his life. People who had known him and were influenced by him left condolences on the web page of the *Kenosha News*. The testimonials conveyed reverence for Howard's kindness. For instance, Ross Guida, the son of an employee at the *Kenosha Daily News*, recounted:

> *I first met Howard when I was a little kid walking around in awe of the whole news operation and how it worked. Howard ALWAYS made time to say hello when I would make my way down to his office and he'd ask how school was going, even when I had grown up and gone away to college and would only make it back every once in a while. If the world had more business owners like Howard who actually put the time in and showed they cared about people on a truly personal level, the world would be a much better place. We'll all miss you, Howard.*

Howard remained the "nice one" throughout his life. As Roger wrote in 2018, just before what would've been his brother's 95th birthday: "Too bad that I didn't have his pleasant personality. He was loved by everyone—even Gene Schulte who took advantage of Howard's kindness. He led a good life and is missed by everyone who knew him." Roger conceded, "Howard's passing is a major event for the Brown family. It makes me feel older, and it is a signal of the beginning of the end. I feel very proud of the traditions of our family, and of the strong relationships that our nieces, our children and our grandchildren have with one another."

MOM'S PRAIRIE

In late spring of 2018, Barbara's health took a turn for the worst. On the morning of her grandson Jacob's wedding, she felt ill enough that Owen drove her to the hospital, where she was admitted and diagnosed with kidney failure. Though unable to attend the ceremony, Barbara still participated in the celebration; Jacob and his new wife, Christine, came to visit her after the event, still dressed in their wedding finery.

After returning home to Highland Park, her health continued to decline. She began dialysis not long after. Three days a week, she and Roger would rise together at 4:45am and drive to her 5:30am dialysis sessions, which limited her capacity to travel. Roger informed the family, "She has decided that she does not want to go to Mexico and will want to move our annual get together to Florida where she believes that there are better dialysis accommodations." She suffered from a series of other ailments: a fistula—which had to be removed surgically—a stomach ulcer, and broken vertebrae. Despite these, she was able to attend the wedding of Aaron Brown and Laura Wood in Chicago, on September 15.

In the winter of 2019, Barbara was medevacked from the family's vacation in Florida back to Highland Park Hospital, where she entered her final illness. "There were pleasant times at the Highland Park Hospital...when family and friends came to wish Barbara well," Roger described her final days, "but the end was in sight." Ariana recalls one of these visits:

Enoch said his favorite memory of Barbara was when we had bagels with cream cheese and lox and French fries at the hospital with her because it was one of the last times he got to see her before she died. As we were leaving, we said goodbye to her at the bedside and she grabbed Aaron's hand in hers, barely able to sit up or talk, and whispered, "Take care." We both left in tears.

In these final visits, Barbara remained committed to her family's well-being. Alison, who spent three days with her in the hospital, recalled, "During my last few days with her at the Highland Park Hospital, she turned to me and said, 'What are you doing here? You've been here three days. Why aren't you at work?' So I flew back to work. She died that first day I was gone."

Roger did not "know why [he] was so shocked when woken on Monday morning to learn that she had passed away." In his first letter after Barbara's death, Roger abandoned his usual composure:

I didn't know if I would ever be able to write a weekly letter again. Mom's death has really unhinged me: and besides suffering from an interminable cough/ cold, I don't know what I'm doing or where I'm going. The standard quote is 'Don't make any big decisions for six months,' but the way I feel now, I don't know what big decisions they are talking about... After 66 years of marriage, it's hard to imagine living alone. I think about Barbara all the time in almost everything I do. I don't think that will change. We had a miraculously good marriage and achieved all the unwritten goals of success... Her love for her family was the building block of her life and its greatest measure of success. They were there for her at the end.

The family stepped up to make necessary arrangements. Andrew had already been in touch with the head of Chicago Jewish Funerals, who helped plan the service. Rabbi Moffic of Congregation Solel, who had known Barbara, led the service. Gail and Andrew hosted Shiva in their home. The mailbox overflowed with letters of condolence; Roger remarked, "that gives me a reason to walk to the mailbox for my daily exercise."

In the weeks that followed Barbara's death, Roger went to several sessions with the North Shore Hospice grievance counselor. "These helped me disclose some of my hidden sins," he wrote. "My problems won't go away; it's a matter of time and being busy doing something." He tried restoring the rhythms of his life, going to concerts, returning to his office at the end of January, having lunch at the Standard Club. By February, Roger wrote to the family in better spirits, even managing some humor:

I am getting used to living alone in this big house... Friends and acquaintances are continuously approaching me and telling me they're sorry. Surprisingly there has been little interest by single women to bring me biscuits etc. I don't think that they are interested in someone who is 93 years old...

It is possible that Owen, Alison and I could take a cruise… In the meantime, I am becoming more aggressive in socializing with older friends.

In the letter he wrote immediately after Barbara's death, Roger mourned her inability to enjoy the house the two of them built together, the grounds—with their orchards and native grasses—that she had cultivated over sixty years: "Too bad that Mom will miss the end of the last chapter in our beautiful home and our glorious garden." In the spring and summer of 2019, Roger himself paid close attention to Barbara's gardens—and updated the family on their status: "Before you go to Northmoor," he wrote to the family in June, "you might want to drive up our driveway and see Mom's prairie—it is starting bloom with some yellow and purple flowers. Maybe you can identify them."

BARBARA'S FIRST SKI TRIP
1954, Colorado

MEXICO

December 2018

The Brown family in Cancun, one of the last times when almost all Brown family members were together

THE BOYS

Thanksgiving 1990, 1261 Clavey Road

Roger & sons after turkey

Chapter 6
EPILOGUE

THIS BIOGRAPHY WAS WRITTEN LARGELY by Aaron Greenberg, who strove graciously through a myriad of delays, comments and suggestions by Roger's headstrong descendants. I occasionally wielded a red pencil to text; more important edits are at the hand of Nicola Brown, whose touch has improved it commensurately. Aaron has asked me, Roger's second son, to write the epilogue.

Most people, glancing back on the general mess and chaos of a life, look hard to find an overwhelming power that had guided their steps. Some believe in fate and a divine hand, others think that they have piloted themselves, on their own strength and recognition, through the shoals of life; it was of their making; they were in control. Roger was having none of that. He more than once told us that his good fortune was due to luck. He meant it. He was grateful for it, and surprised.

This does not mean that our father was not better qualified, by experience, character and education, than most. Nor in his daily life did he rely only on fortune's grace. Rather, while planning for success, he also tried in general to guess what might go wrong, and if it did, how he could compensate. He had the humility to believe that all this preparation was as little compared to what events the world might serve. In good and in bad, he presented to that world a face of equanimity.

This before both triumph and failure. This biography chronicles his accomplishments as a businessman; less obvious are his failures. There was, for example, an insurance business with Isidore which, through no fault of their own, dragged them through the courts for years. Never a word on this to the family. There was the Lloyd's Reinsurance debacle of the '80's, with Barbara an outside investing "Name," that is, a passive source of capital with unlimited liability for loss, and "Names," because of lax, stupid, or fraudulent underwriting, facing personal bankruptcy. Of which he told me "I'll just go out and make some more money."

He believed, perhaps, that if you were always on top you were too cautious, and as long as your batting average was positive, then you could investigate interesting nooks and crannies of the investment world—GE a few years ago, Tontine and Grafton right after the turn of the century, oil shale in the early '90's, nuclear fusion in the '70's (yes, kids, he put money into that) and no one now alive knows what debacles he spent his wealth on before then. Rest assured that there were probably catastrophes aplenty, just not nearly so many as there were really good investments.

He also said that such disasters can bring out the best in people. What you believe shapes how you act, and Roger believed people could do well. Although he was by nature a pessimist (he would say a realist), he also felt that in general people could be counted on to be altruistic, and to care not just for themselves, but for others. He did, and he believed it his duty (although he would be too modest to say such) to maintain and better society. While enriching himself and his family, he at the same time wished to mitigate poverty and desperation, no matter where in these United States this was found. He found himself funding out of his own pocket, and later through the I & G, ventures that aided prisoners, the mentally ill or challenged, impoverished children, Native Americans, drug users in recovery, Jews in need, and scores of similar efforts to repair the world.

This is not to paint Roger a saint. He was good to his staff. He loved his family. Yet he was domineering to the point, sometimes, that they didn't always love him back. He believed in a social contract but was ever more distrustful of government. After Charles Percy, there were few politicians he liked; Donald Rumsfeld's tenure as Secretary of Defense, who he had hired at Becker, was perhaps his greatest disappointment. But he felt that you should do what you could to make what you touch a bit better, and that although life's end is tragic, one can always enjoy oneself before then. This he set out to do. Many of his years in retirement (although when did he ever retire?) were happy ones.

Now he lives alone, at 1261. Barbara is gone, and his strength, both physical and cognitive, has dimmed. "I am not what once I was," he told me a few months ago. He also told me he knew what his end would be. Still, he said, he was ready to step up. To what, I don't know.

We chatted today, two days before the 2020 presidential election. I mentioned the race, he told me he was glad he was out of it, and hoped Trump would be soon, too. I told him that I was writing this epilogue, and he laughed. I asked him whether he recalled mentioning Rumsfeld to me, and he said "he might have." I went over some of the ideas he had bred within us, a belief in not only the individual, but an individual's place in society—the need for purposefulness and for financial independence, the give and take between autonomy and a healthy, just community. "Sounds complicated!" he said. "But write what you want. I am going to take a nap."

I do know that at some time, somewhere, and if only faintly, Roger felt that there was a door into an earthly paradise. Putting aside his everyday, self-focused pleasures, in skiing and tennis, in Veuve Cliquot and Mom's cooking, in travel and the reflected glow of his children and grandchildren's accomplishments, he believed a world possible where more people were givers than takers. This was a far-off goal, one he barely expressed, and which only an acute observer could recognize in him, but I suspect his generosity to others was motivated by pursuit of it. Hardly achievable, and then only fleeting, but worth the chase, just as the pursuit of wealth was worth pursuing. This was a feeling Roger seldom spoke of, but when he did, he meant it.

Perhaps that is his most important belief for us, perhaps that is his most important legacy.

— OWEN BROWN
November 2020

HALLEY'S COMET

Autumn 1986

*Barbara & Roger host a family trip
to the Southwest for the occasion.*

SELECTED LETTERS

Roger, dear:

Mother and I have given serious thought
to what would be an appropriate gift for your graduation,
one that will symbolize our profound love and confidence
in you and reflect our understanding of each other. After much consideration we came to the decision that the
content of this message would be a most significant gift.
We hope you agree.

Commencement has many connotations - it
brings joy to some, sadness to others and indifference
to many. To us it indicates not a severance from what
you have been doing, but a jointure with what you are
about to commence to do.

We confess that perhaps our generation
did a poor job in the past by permitting itself to become fat, feeble and lazy, thereby growing weak and
overindulgent enough to permit an evil system to grow
up in the world which was the cause and forerunner of
World War II. We have thus given youth a heavy burden
to bear. But some of us of strength and character still
remain to keep the faith, to adjust and remedy our er -
rors. And do it we must.

Your generation is faced with the most
solemn task and courageous duty that man has ever been
challenged to meet. Also you have the greatest opportunity to create a new order that will prevent a reoc-
currence of our past blunders. Only men of great vi -
sion and integrity will be able to cope with and solve
these problems. As our generation passes on and loses
its grip, yours will be expected to hold on more vigor-
ously and with greater determination.

Schools in their greater aspect, are
character builders. They lead one out of the darkness
into the light and help one distinguish the good from
the wicked. Spiritually, as well as socially, they set
the pace and path for the well being of the student.
Our greatest difficult has been our failure to recognize
that we are "our brothers' keeper." This resulted in
isolationism and led to the present chaos and conflagra-
tion.

From the strong moral fibre that youth
possesses combined with our experience, there will be
formulated a new thought and philosophy that should prevent future wars. Yes, dear son, this seems difficult
but it is all possible, if the nations of the world which,
in the final analysis, consist of individual human beings,
will strive to break down the present economic barriers
and aim to provide sufficient room and equal opportunity
for all. Nations must also strengthen their belief in the
"brotherhood of man." This will abolish the prejudices
that now exist between races, creeds and religions.

Now you are commencing to go out into the
world and to apply those principles and standards of dealing with your neighbors, as you have applied in living har-
moniously with your room-mate - - to practice the theory
of unselfishness, to recognize the problem that the good
that one does lives after him and the goal that he seeks
should not be self centered, but contributed to humanity
in its broadest and finest sense.

Certainly your book lore and your under -
standing of the sciences and fine arts will help you appreciate and recognize these objectives more clearly,
but the most important objective of all is your application of the "golden rule," and your desire to live peacefully, justly and unselfishly.

We have an abiding faith and conviction
in you and your success. We know that you are prepared
to meet these contingencies and we assure you that we
w'll keep the faith with your generation to the extent
that we are willing to be held responsible for our de-
faults and to be led by youth's intelligence and inge-
nuity.

The elders acknowledge their insolvency
and recognize that youth is now on trial to determine
whether it is prepared and ready to sacrifice enough
for the purpose of creating a new and better plan and
program of living; whether it is aware of its potential
strength to accept leadership; for the decision of the
world now rests in youth's hands.

This commencement should represent a
combination of things known and a keen anticipation and
desire to accept and learn things unknown.

#3..

We congratulate you on your many accomplishments; we live in the hope and expectation of
witnessing you gain even greater honors, and finally
we wish for you that inner peace and happiness that
comes through the satisfaction of knowing that only
those things that are true, beautiful and of good report are worth striving for and achieving. Time is
short, spend it well.

Your devoted and loving parents.

July 1, 1943

My Dear Son Roger:

> "No coward soul is mine,
> No trembler in the world's storm-troubled sphere:
> I see Heaven's glories shine,
> And Faith shines equal, arming me from fear."
>
> E. Bronte.

The time is now rapidly approaching when you will be given the privilege of taking up arms to defend your Country. This is a new adventure and I hope you will live it nobly.

In the first instance, your Government is sending you to an institution of higher learning rather than directly to a battle field. This is another demonstration of the thought, care and consideration that the democracy you are fighting for gives to its citizens. The respect and dignity with which your Government clothes you will undoubtedly be reflected in your devotion to its noble principles and in the valiant service that you will render. Soldiering is a worthy career and has been the lot of many of the most celebrated and distinguished men of this Country.

In this new walk of life you will meet strange characters and new faces, each representing a personality all its own, each having his individual peculiarities. People learn the meaning of life from the groups in which they live and from their contact with every facet of opinion. Meet each new acquaintance in the attitude of friendliness and with the feeling that he has a great deal of good in him and in the expectancy that you will become fond of him. No two people will react the same towards your ideas and habits - - each has a right to his opinion and you must respect these opinions regardless of whether they coincide with yours.

Your rank, station or position in civilian life is now a closed chapter and should temporarily be stored away in some recess of your mind to be revived and refreshed after your discharge from the service.

You did not descend from a tribe or family
of warriors. Your people love peace. The trunk of
the tree from which you emanate represents ancient
lineage, splendid tradition and fine heritage. Think
of this in your line of duty and use it well, for it
will be a great fountain of comfort, strength and
courage to you.

It should not be difficult to impress you
that it is a great honor to serve your Country in time
of war as well as in time of peace. Those who are
physically or mentally unfit stand on the side lines
in longing admiration of those who actively participate. While your dad is beyond the age limit, he is
proud of the fact that he is able to measure his contribution to Victory by his sons' achievements.

In a sense you are making a great sacrifice
and yet you are only proving your right to American cit-
izenship; you are redeeming your oft repeated pledge of
allegiance to Old Glory.

Be alert and vigilant. Keep your service
on the highest and most idealistic plane. Do not permit any order or instruction to escape you and do not
side-step or dodge the performance of these orders regardless of how menial or arduous. Keep your ears at-
tuned to the movement and progress of the Navy and be
inspired by the history and tradition of our famous
Navy and its gallant heroes.

In this letter I say nothing about devotion
to cause, patriotism, the four freedoms, etc. I omit
these intentionally because at home and in the respec-
tive institutions that you have attended you have been
so well grounded to have faith in these doctrines that
repitition would be vain and superfluous.

Now that you are engaged in the holiest
crusade, let your thoughts be pure, your acts effective, your words few - Come back a better man, pur-
ified through the crucible of sweat, tears and blood.
"Peace hath her victories no less renown than War."
Go forward to retain your heritage and to prove your
unassailable right to share the glory of being an
American.

GOD BLESS YOU.

7 January 1947

Dear Folks,

I hope that you are all well rested and had an interesting voyage to Boca. I advise mother to rest her cold until all symptoms have disappeared. It is time that she realize though she may not admit that she is past thirty.

Howard and I had an enjoyable lunch at the Polachecks. We had hot apple strudel for desert which would have made the chef at Voisin's drool for joy, it was so good. We had an interesting talk with the Polachecks after we pierced through their constant bickering about small insignificant details. Howard and I finally brought to earth our arguments concerning education. I think that Howard's ad argument was more impressive, and naturally more eloquent, but mine is right from every conceiveable angle. Mr. Polacheck is a very wise man who has made a fortune through his own intelligence, hard work and energy. His whole life has been based on two strong feelings: the belief that he was created on earth for some purpose, and a strong, artistic interest in metal work. These two feelings were so strong that they were able to combine and build him a fortune from nothing. I am afraid that he is a fish out of water. He is a man who needs to have hard work well-organized for its accomplishment, and his life of retirement has brought him to believe that he has lost the abilities that he used to have. His wife appears to be almost a detriment to him at this time of life, as she is over-emotional, and rather small in her outlook. However, how can I really look behind the scenes in their life so that I can realize or understand the part that she plays in it. I may be approaching the whole aspect from the wrong angle who can tell.

Howard and I saw Buddy Cummings again before we left the Waldorf. She is one of th most interesting women that I know, mainly because I can't understand her. Her intonations and actions are supremely kind and sincere, but it is hard to believe that a person can mean all the things that she says, and not say the things that she feels -- or does she feel them. The woman is really an enigma to me. What motivates her? She is either the world's worst hypocrite or a saint. I suppose that we are all hypocrites, for none of us really knows what he wants.

I caught the seven o! clock out of New York, and I arrived in New Haven last night. I went to my room

and began to consider the prospects of the coming six
months. The feeling of returning to school was terrible. No matter what I say or do I realize that I am
not a student, and I do not enjoy studying. I would
prefer the wild rich boys happy life of college. I
have not devel#oped the temperment of asking questions
and getting answers. I can look at things from a distance and say that I think it would be enjoyable to do
a certain thing, but in the long run I find that my x
will has no control over my mind or body. I choose x
the source of least resistence with a constant realization that I am xx doing the wrong thing. I can
think of no time in my life during which I have accomplished a worthwhile task by beginning it, and continuing it, and finishing it with a constant push of energy in which I unfold all the blind alleys. I may
start with a burst of enthusiasm or end with a burst
of necessity; but seldom do I do a good job and hardly ever my best. I am coming to the realization that
I am in school mainly kx so that I shall force myself
through the means of a third party to get a decent education so that I shall have an understanding of the
world I live in and some of the benefits that civilization can offer. I am not doing what I would like
to do, though I feel that I am doing something that
is valuable and something that I wish I would like to
do. My main drawback is that I DO NOT KNOW WHAT I
WANT TO DO, AND IF I DID KNOW WHAT I WANTED TO DO, I
WOULD NOT KNOW WHY I SHOULD DO IT. I am alwys being
thwarted by the constant questioning of why -- why do
we have a will to live? why do we have an ego that
seeks prestige? why do we enjoy certain sensual pleasures?
why do we hate our fellow man? why was such an extremely delicate organism created? is there a purpose in
life? John Polacheck was a success in life because he
had a purpose (or thought he had one), and this realization of this purpose drove him xxxxx out of his
father's house and out of Hungary to the United States.
I am as intelligent as John Polacheck, I am better educated than he was, and I already have been given an
incipient fortune; but I don't have the drive and the
inner makings that he had, or at least I have not realized them within the last twenty-one years.

        We are now approaching the crux of the issue.
What can I do that will give me the opportunity to
make the most of myself as a person? The best way to
begin answering this question is kx to consider the
immediate future. Should I continue my work as a
special student at Yale? At the present moment I am
inclined to think I should continue as I am, my strong-
est reason being that it is something that I started
and therefore I should finish it. The easiest way of
finishing it, is by continuing at Yale. Should I go
to Harvard Business School? I intend to xxx send in

an application, but at the present moment I do not
intend to go to Harvard, because I think that going
there would just be a delay in time, and it would not
help to inculcate the necessary drive or feeling of
purpose that are necessary for success. I therefore
expect to go to work in the summer of 1947, the big
question remaining is what kind of work should I do
and who should I work for. I cannot answer the first
question as yet. I intend to get a job with a concern that is the leader in its field, but which also
offers opportunities for individualism and advancement. I want to learn the industry from the biggest
and the best, and then when the opportunity comes along,
I want to step out and work for myself. I hope you
save this letter as I would like to read it in three or
four months, at which time I may have a different x
point of view.

My valise arrived safe and sound, and my room
looked much more cheerful than my returning eyes dared
to picture it. Everything seems to be in ship-shape
order, and as yet I have run into no difficulties ex-
cept that I had to pay an additional $23e10 to the
Waldorf as they charged us for our room on the third
of January and they would not refund the money because they said that the room had to be held for our
occupancy on the 3rd. I think that their reasoning
is fallacious, but apparently we were playing a game
under their rules and had to abide by what they said.
I have x written a memo to Col. Lang to let him know
that I only have $1400 in my banking account for the
payment of my income tax; I also asked him for an item-
ized account of my earnings and deductions for income
tax purposes.

                          Love,

                          Roger

Yale University

15 January 1947

Dear Folks,

This is to let you know that I received the four
letters that Dad has sent to me from Florida. Their
receipt was certainly a surprise to me, for I had not
expected that the short note that I sent you was so
stirring. I intend to answer the letters you sent me
within a week, but at the present time I am almost
drowning in work, and exams are coming up next week.
Therefore I hope that this short note will serve to
show my intentions without souring your expectations.
Otherwise there is very little news outside of the
ordinary babble, and I hope that everything is all
right with you in sunny Fla.

Love,

March 14, 1983

Dear Everyone,

We have been fortunate to have Henry visiting us at home this week.
He leaves early next Wednesday for Washington and more job interviews.
A couple of days ago he had both his upper and lower wisdom teeth on his
right side pulled. He is still in a bit of pain but it is decreasing.
He has the teeth and we are looking forward to an electron microscopic
photo of the villains.

What an unusual set of circumstances. Three of our sons are looking
for jobs -- and what a terrible time to be released to a stuttering economy
where businesses don't want to pay for business school graduates and many
are still in a contraction phase, cutting back on employment so that their
costs can be competitive. It's never pleasant looking for jobs and now is
even a more trying time. As bad as it is think of those personnel people
who have to interview all the applicants and can give them little or no
hope. Regardless, talent will emerge and regardless of what you think
you want to do now or where you want to work, you will eventually get
employed and that will be a grand beginning to a career that will lead
into many paths none of which can now be predicted. Somehow your skills
will be utilized -- but they will be your basic skills -- those that deal
with understanding human nature and the culture in which you are working.
Most of the specific technical skills you have accumulated will begin to
atrophy as their need is diminished though they will remain in your deep
memory to be recalled and polished for action if and when the time comes.
Your job will require new techniques and your past ability to accumulate
knowledge will be very helpful. Keep trying, persist, you will succeed.
Don't expect anything to drop in your lap even though it might.

After spending two weekends in a row traveling out of town Mom and
I are both happy to be home relaxing over this weekend. I felt particularly
tired this week. Part of it may be the seasonal compensation problems at
Harris Associates, but there are also the transitional problems of our
business that has expanded much faster than we anticipated in the advisory
segment of our business and is contracting much faster than we expected
in the options area of our business. Handling these changes requires skills
which will test me to the extreme, but I think I can manage it with the
right type of assistance. Through all this I have some good news and that is
I have hired a new secretary. Margaret Curry who spent 15 years at A. G.
Becker and worked there for my good friend, Ken Nelson. Marge starts on
Tuesday and will be "shown the ropes" by Laura as Laura concentrates
on finishing the work on our taxes in 1982. Marlene Halperin, who under
Laura's guidance has been doing bookkeeping, auditing, and tax preparation
for many of our different accounts will continue with this work and hopefully
will pick up some additional work. Somehow or another it will all be
figured out.

Yesterday we saw the movie <u>The Year of Living Dangerously</u> about an Australian news broadcaster who is sent to Indonesia on his first important foreign assignment. It is during the end of Sukarno's reign in a period when the local communist party is attempting to wrest control away from the military. On arriving in Djakarta the Australian meets and teams up with a half-Chinese dwarf as a camera man. The dwarf is a Tolstoyan figure who can't resolve the problem of wealthy people co-existing with poverty and disease. His solution is fighting the system, which ends in suicide. This is the basic question of the film - "what should we do" to prevent and solve these problems. Of course it is not answered in Indonesia any better than it is answered in any other undeveloped country. Their cultures do not seem to be able to cope with "Western" ideas of wealthy societies in the near term. The turn-around time may take centuries. There is much hope -- witness the development in Brazil, Korea, Signapore, Malaysia, Mexico and India. Most of Africa seems to be impossible - and the OPEC countries will revert quickly as the price of oil collapses. This is an interesting film with a torrid romance having nothing to do with the real plot.

Love,

P.S. I forgot to mention that we heard the Symphony on Friday night after dinner with the Foremans and Honigbergs. The performance of Die Meistersingers was unusually good, but unfortunately I slept through too much of it.

186

ABOUT THE TYPE

SABON
8/10/11PT ROMAN

This is a beloved, old-style serif typeface designed by Jan Tschichold in the late 1960s. The type was inspired by Claude Garamond (c. 1480–1561) and named after French designer Jacques Sabon (c.1580-1590), who inherited much of Garamond's collection. A coalition of German printers commissioned Sabon to create a classic typeface that could be printed identically on Linotype, Monotype, or letterpress equipment, thus simplifying the process of book printing. The italic styles are restrained by Linotype casting machines, requiring the character widths of each letter to match between styles, giving the italic its characteristic narrow *f*.